Buffaloes by My Bedroom

Tales of Tanganyika

Buffaloes by My Bedroom

Tales of Tanganyika

Dennis Herlocker

iUniverse, Inc.
New York　Bloomington

Buffaloes by My Bedroom
Tales of Tanganyika

Copyright © 2009 by Dennis Jon Herlocker

All rights reserved. No part of this book may be used or reproduced by any means, graphic, electronic, or mechanical, including photocopying, recording, taping or by any information storage retrieval system without the written permission of the publisher except in the case of brief quotations embodied in critical articles and reviews.

iUniverse books may be ordered through booksellers or by contacting:

iUniverse
1663 Liberty Drive
Bloomington, IN 47403
www.iuniverse.com
1-800-Authors (1-800-288-4677)

Because of the dynamic nature of the Internet, any Web addresses or links contained in this book may have changed since publication and may no longer be valid. The views expressed in this work are solely those of the author and do not necessarily reflect the views of the publisher, and the publisher hereby disclaims any responsibility for them.

ISBN: 978-1-4401-4724-1 (pbk)
ISBN: 978-1-4401-4725-8 (ebk)
ISBN: 978-1-4401-4726-5(cloth)

Library of Congress Control Number: 2009929222

Printed in the United States of America
iUniverse rev. date: 6/12/09

This book is for my parents, who encouraged me to start it; Aunt Alice "Where's the next chapter?" Evans, who ensured I finished it; and Cathy, who put up with me in the meantime. Many thanks.

Table of Contents

Acknowledgments	ix
List of Figures	xi
Introduction	xiii

Getting There
Getting Ready	1
Arrival and First Impressions	7
On to Ngorongoro	19

Getting Started
The First Day	27
Finally to Work	42

Colleagues, Elephants, and Game-viewing Tracks
The Conservators	51
The Buffalo Ridge Track	57
The Wildlife Biologist	64
The Gorgor Swamp Track	70
How Not to View an Elephant	78
The Game Scouts and Their Boss	83

Life on the Crater Rim
Buffaloes by My Bedroom	92
A Welcome Visitor	103

Forest Patrols and Grass Fires
Bee Hives and Elephant Trails	110
Trespassers in the Forest	123
Grass Fires	131

Plains, Craters, and People

Welcoming Herman to Africa	142
Some Crater Happenings	151
Letters from Cathy	161
The Empakaai Crater Safari	166
A Serengeti Game Count	183
Time to Go Home	193
Scientific Names of Selected Plant Species	203
Bibliography and Further Reading	204
Glossary	205

Acknowledgments

Thanks are due to Christy Myers, Frank Payne, Wayne Werbel, Steve and Yvonne Stephenson, Larry Harris, Herman Dirschl, Jeff Gottfried, George Frame, Lory Herbison Frame (editorial consultant), Richard D. Estes, and David Anstey for providing encouragement, advice, information, and other forms of assistance.

List of Figures

Cover photo: Buffalo in a stand of fever trees

1. Map of Africa showing the location of Tanganyika — 5
2. Map of Tanganyika showing features mentioned in the book — 13
3. Maasai women. — 15
4. Market at Mtu wa Mbu. — 25
5. Map of Ngorongoro Crater — 31
6. Maasai *boma* — 32
7. A view of Ngorongoro Crater — 34
8. Map of the Ngorongoro Conservation Area — 40
9. Henry Fosbrooke and Mr. Mlangai in tree plantation — 54
10. John Goddard and game scout Tsitote — 68
11. An elephant at the edge of Lerai Forest — 91
12. Game scout Sambegi on a sand dune in the Salei Plain — 91
13. My house. — 95
14. A traditional Maasai warrior or murrani — 102
15. A modern Maasai: Philip ole Sayalel. — 102
16. Cathy Lange. — 109
17. A grass fire on the floor of Ngorongoro Crater — 149
18. The author and Herman Dirschl at Endulen — 150
19. Marking a captured wildebeest in Ngorongoro Crater — 154
20. Lake Emakat and the volcano Oldoinyo Lengai — 173
21. Looking south from Empakaai Crater — 181
22. Wildebeest and zebra on the eastern Serengeti Plains — 191
23. Maasai warriors watching the refueling of an airplane in Ngorongoro Crater — 191

Introduction

In 1964, when I was 27, the U.S. Peace Corps asked me if I wanted to use my considerable experience as a forester—all three years of it—to help a newly independent nation get on its feet. The nation was Tanganyika and apparently it needed all the help it could get. Now, it so happened that I knew something about the place. Indeed, the name "Tanganyika" conjured up visions of romance and adventure: snowy Mt. Kilimanjaro, for instance, rising high above grassy savannas dotted with wild game; migrating herds of wildebeest and zebra on the Serengeti Plains; spear-carrying warriors guarding their cattle; safaris—that romantic Swahili word meaning journey—and, and, and ... I accepted the offer and never regretted it.

Tanganyika, previously a United Nations Trust Territory administered by the British government, was in a state of political transition. Africans were taking over high-level governmental positions, and many British, either unable or unwilling to stay on, were leaving. However, there weren't enough qualified Tanganyikan citizens to replace them, so volunteers from North America and Europe were helping to keep the government running until Africans were trained to take over.

I was one of those volunteers, occupying the position of assistant conservator (forests) with the Ngorongoro Conservation Unit in the north of the country. I loved the job. It included a level of responsibility that would have taken several years to attain back home. The setting of volcanic mountains and craters, abrupt escarpments, grassy plains, and highland forests was stunning; encounters with wild animals were an everyday experience. The local people lived as they had hundreds of years ago, and my associates were an intriguing cultural mix of Europeans, North Americans, Indians (from the Indian subcontinent), and Africans. Furthermore, it was during this time that I met, courted, and married my wife. The three years at Ngorongoro were the most enjoyable of my life. It was a wonderful time in a wonderful place, a world that hitherto, I had dreamed about but never hoped to experience.

These stories are based on real people, places, and events. Although diary entries, library research, and cherished memories (to the extent these are reliable after four decades) provide the book's factual backbone, imagination and artistic license filled some gaps, for example dialogue.

The Swahili words and sentences that crop up throughout the book are often not *safi*, or pure, Swahili, but the simpler "upcountry" version which I eventually learned to speak—sort of. The Swahili prefix "Wa," indicating a tribe or people, is used here when a tribe's name might otherwise be confused with a major landmark (Warusha people and Arusha Town, for instance), or when it is spoken by a native Swahili speaker. Locally accepted spellings have been used for tribal and place names—Maasai rather than Masai, Oldupai Gorge rather than Olduvai Gorge, etc. The fact that I was able to communicate with the local people at all owes much to their patience and good manners. Almost without exception, they were the better linguists, speaking Swahili as well as one or more tribal languages, usually some English, and occasionally French.

Tanganyika no longer exists because about a year after I arrived, it merged with Zanzibar and took on a new name: Tanzania. Four decades later, this change of names finally impinged on me when I discovered some of my stories to have happened in Tanganyika and others in Tanzania. I decided to stick to the original name. Partly, this was because the people and institutions were still essentially Tanganyikan in nature, the new entity of Tanzania having yet to mark them with its unique stamp. However, it was also because Tanganyika, Swahili for *Sails in the Wilderness*, seems the more-interesting of the two names.

Getting There

Getting Ready

The man tramping through the forest ahead of me, a forest guard named Hai, suddenly stiffened. A second later, he exclaimed something in his native tongue, whipped around and rushed past me so fast he almost knocked me over.

Then I saw it: partly hidden in the shrubs, a large, black, massively-horned African buffalo, staring at me with murderous intent. And it was only twenty feet away! Easing behind a large shrub, I turned and began to slowly retreat.

Behind me there was an explosive snort, thudding hooves, and the sound of a large animal crashing through dense bush. I stopped tiptoeing and started running; bouncing off tree trunks, leveling bushes, and getting my face whipped by branches; tearing through the forest like it wasn't there. Later, after we learned the buffalo had actually fled from, rather than chased us, the forest guards kidded me about the speed of my retreat. They said they had never seen a white bwana run so fast—this from two guys who had been so far ahead of me that, despite my best efforts, I trailed them by thirty yards.

The next day, cradling a cup of steaming tea in my hands, I looked out the window of my little house and admired a view fit for a travel poster. Before me, a full two thousand feet lower in elevation, lay Ngorongoro, an eleven-mile-wide crater inhabited by thousands of African game animals. Dark mountains rose beyond it from a high plateau, the inverted image of one reflecting in the unnaturally still waters of a shallow lake on the crater floor. Almost in the center of this dramatic backdrop, close to the house, two waterbuck grazed beside an ancient-looking nuxia tree. Once again I wondered at my luck in being posted here.

I'd been attracted to the Peace Corps ever since its inception four years earlier in 1961. I liked the idea of volunteering, and wanted to see the world. Anywhere would do, but Tanganyika in East Africa was especially attractive because my Dad had always wanted to visit that country's world-famous Serengeti Plains and Ngorongoro Crater. The Great Depression and family responsibilities kept him from traveling, but he never lost his interest. He also imparted it to me.

A forester, I spent my days tramping through forests of fir, hemlock, and cedar, working to the quiet patter of rain, the creak and groan of trees massaged by the wind, and the sudden *thump-thump-thump* of deer in surprised retreat. At first, I enjoyed it. But the work eventually became routine and I began to feel the social isolation of a single man in a small rural town where most people were married. Then the Peace Corps recruiters came to a nearby city and I wondered if maybe this was it—my chance to get overseas. I signed up.

Of course, I might not be accepted. I had even less confidence about being sent to Africa, much less Tanganyika, my first choice. Therefore, I was pleasantly surprised when the Peace Corps mailed me a large envelope. Then, after opening it and discovering that I'd had been accepted for a posting in southern Tanganyika, I jumped around pumping the air like a frenetic cheer leader. Tanganyika! Now I'd be able to see Ngorongoro Crater and the Serengeti, at least once.

Eighty-four other volunteers and I trained at an eastern university. Our group, Tanganyika V, was a mix of professionals ranging from agriculturists and engineers to nurses and lawyers. Many of us were to fill positions within the Tanganyika civil service vacated by British staff departing after Tanganyika's independence. For example, the five foresters were destined for the Tanganyika Village Resettlement Program, which was centralizing widely scattered farmers in villages in order to provide them with water, electricity, health care, and security. We were to help plan, survey, and build these settlements.

The training included lectures on the culture, history, and geography of Tanganyika, bits and pieces of which have remained with me to this day.

"You probably think that Africans are unfamiliar with democracy," stated the neatly bearded professor. "In fact, village elders typically debate issues for hours, or even days, until everyone agrees. Everyone!"

"We Americans believe that progress is inherently good," pronounced the anthropologist. "But there is often a downside. For instance, African parents may see no progress in educating their children if this removes them from helping on the farm and tending the herds."

"Look at that walking stick," muttered my neighbor in the large, steeply tiered lecture hall. I was already looking. Made of ebony, it had a large D-ring handle and strange-looking African figures carved on it. It belonged to our guest lecturer, an African Member of Parliament from Tanganyika, who dressed and spoke like a graduate of a British public school. Were other politicians in Tanganyika the same appealing mix of African and Western cultures? I looked forward to finding out.

Those of us destined for village resettlement and public works positions also studied basic surveying and construction. The latter was the most interesting course because as a practical exercise we built a wooden bridge. In a nearby forest, the men energetically felled trees, lopped branches, peeled and notched logs, and did other manly things, while a group of woman volunteers, all nurses, stood around hoping for an accident to happen. They too were doing their practical.

Their wish almost came true. The bridge was to have concrete abutments. Once the wooden forms were up, we called in a cement truck. While it was chugging away pouring the concrete, we put on knee-length rubber boots and hopped down to spread the concrete evenly with shovels. When the level rose to a certain point we hopped back out again—except for one man. This guy was so immersed in his work that he carried on spreading concrete while continuing a now one-sided conversation with people who weren't there any more; only when the concrete began pouring over the tops of his boots did he yell for help. We pulled him out but his boots remained behind. If the abutments are ever broken up for whatever purpose, whoever discovers those boots is going to wonder where the body is buried.

But the days were sunny, the forest was shady, and everyone was in good spirits. The only blot on the scene was our instructor who tended, we thought, to interfere. What we wanted was the occasional "Well done!" or "Bravo!" from the sidelines but what we got was him right in amongst us pointing out the problems. "Who's responsible for this missing nut? Wedge that log tighter; you want the bridge to collapse? Gentlemen, this bridge won't support a starving goat much less a herd of elephants!" The last straw came late one afternoon when the crew put what we considered the final touches on the bridge. Finally, it was done. Furthermore, it looked good, well able to take the next herd of elephants to pass this way. We were standing there feeling proud of ourselves, certain now that we could handle anything Tanganyika could throw at us, when we realized that our instructor, whom we had momentarily forgotten, was talking. "Two planks replaced ... log re-bored ... abutment chipped ... alignment off ... must be ... *Before this bridge is done!*" Stunned to silence we just gaped at him. Then I was pulled to one side by the group and the following conversation ensued:

Buffaloes by My Bedroom

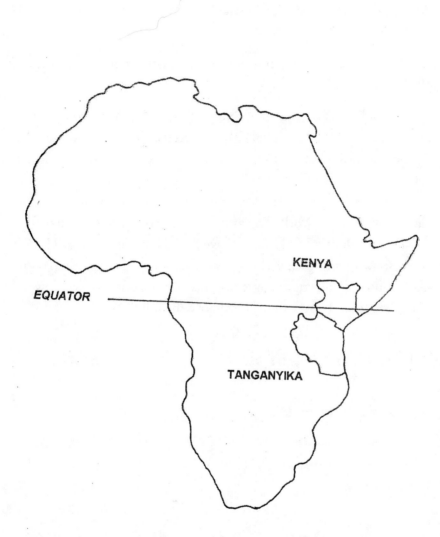

Map of Africa showing the location of Tanganyika

"Dennis, you're old." I was all of twenty-seven

"You're diplomatic." I'm a good listener.

"Go over there and tell that so-and-so to get the blankety-blank off our bridge!"

Our instructor then demonstrated his maturity by not kicking us off the program.

To celebrate the end of training, Tanganyika V toured Boston, traveling there by bus through Massachusetts. With us was Nigel, an engineer who was part of the training team. Raised in postwar Britain before the advent of dual carriageways, he was used to the narrow, winding, up-and-down lanes of England. A road engineer for the Tanganyika Public Works Department, he was equally familiar with the dirt and *murram* (a kind of gravel) roads of Tanganyika. He had never seen anything like the freeways cutting through the rolling Massachusetts landscape. Flattening his nose against his window, he muttered, "Bloody hell, they just remove the hills!"

I sincerely hoped that what he considered normal and mundane in Tanganyika would be as fascinating to us as our highways were to him.

Arrival and First Impressions

A buzz of excited voices filled the plane. As flight attendants moved along the aisle ensuring passengers fastened their seat belts, I looked out at the coast of Tanganyika. It was a lovely scene, the deep blue of the Indian Ocean changing to a translucent light green near white beaches fringed with palm trees. We were close enough that I could pick out scattered hamlets and villages and, here and there, small plantations of trees. Tin roofs glinted in the sun. The plane, its wings noticeably waggling as its air speed slowed, continued its descent. Suddenly a beach with boats drawn up on it flashed beneath us. Then trees; then large flat-topped buildings; then lawns, then trees, more thatched huts; then a road with pedestrians and bicyclists; then more houses, more roads: We were almost there.

Our British Overseas Air Co. Comet jet liner landed at Dar es Salaam Airport and taxied to a halt in front of the terminal. Ground staff rolled a portable stairway up to the plane and we emerged, bleary-eyed and rumpled, into bright sunlight and warm, humid air. Shuffling into the nearly empty terminal building, we had our first taste of Africa: barring ourselves and a few senior officials of Indian (from the Indian subcontinent) and European (white people) origin, everyone—officials, staff, onlookers—was African. My next experience was finding that my suitcase had been misplaced. For the time being I would have to continue wearing what I had on, wrinkled and smelly though it was. I hoped this was not an omen of things to come.

Buses took us to the Mgulani Salvation Army Camp in the southern suburbs where we were to stay until our postings were finalized. The camp, shaded by palm trees, was large and grassy. Masses of colorful Bougainvillea draped its perimeter walls, flowering in red, pink, and white. Frangipani bloomed and jasmine scent filled the air. Smiling, uniformed African staff served us tea as we relaxed in the open at benched tables, watching a hazy sunset. I forgot about my rumpled, odoriferous clothes.

The next morning I was up with the sun, smelling flowers, watching birds, and listening to the chatter of Swahili among the African staff. At breakfast, which included two firsts for me—fresh pineapples and papayas (*papaws*)—my immediate neighbors seemed unaware of the unwashed state of my clothing. One was squeezing lemon juice over his papaya; the other was feeding bread crumbs to some brilliantly feathered birds on the grass. Directly across from me, an attractive nurse from Philadelphia stared straight ahead with unfocused eyes as she poured an amber stream of tea onto the table near her teacup—she wasn't even awake yet. I shifted her cup under the stream of tea.

"Cathy, it's full, you can stop pouring now."

Of all the female volunteers, Cathy was the one I liked best. Not only was she pretty, but also quiet, self-contained, and serious. Maybe, once she woke up and recognized me, we could—a loud hail from across the compound broke my reverie, and I remembered that I had already agreed to go into town with someone else today.

"You want taxi?" The slightly built African with a pork pie hat motioned invitingly towards a small British car parked near the Mgulani Camp gate. We hesitated. It didn't look like a taxi. There was no sign that said taxi. It wasn't painted yellow or in black checks and it lacked a meter. A hubcap was missing and the right rear window was cracked. All in all, it exhibited decidedly untaxi-like attributes. However, it seemed to be the only transport around, so we took the plunge. The driver opened the taxi door from the inside—"It is broke," he explained—and we crowded into the back. We were greeted by a large African woman dressed in brightly colored *kitenge* cloth who was occupying the front seat.

"*Hamjambo*," she smiled, revealing teeth like polished white piano keys. Is nothing wrong with you?

"*Hatujambo, Mama*," we replied. Nothing is wrong with us.

The driver engaged gears and off we went ... down the "wrong" side of the road. It was some time before I stopped leaning to the right, subconsciously trying to get the driver to change lanes.

"She not speak English," said the driver, referring to his female passenger. Therefore, we focused on him, eager to take advantage of our first opportunity to communicate at length with a real African. He was James, a Chagga from the slopes of Mt. Kilimanjaro, and an active though unofficial member of the Chaggaland Chamber of Commerce. Proudly James told us about how educated and modern the Wachagga (the tribe's Swahili name) were: they had the only coffee growers cooperative in the country; the newest technical training institute; the most teachers, government officials, and businessmen.... "We the most progressive peoples in country," he declared.

At this point, the woman passenger, who had become increasingly restive during James's oration, intervened. Drawing herself up, she glared at the driver. Her eyes flashed. Her chin jutted. Then she hosed James with a torrent of angry-sounding Swahili to which, after a brief hesitation, he responded in kind. For a few minutes, they argued vigorously and loudly until James remembered he was contending with a paying customer, and the noise subsided. For a few minutes, we drove in silence, the woman resentful, the driver thoughtful. Finally, his eyes blank of all expression, he spoke to us again. "The Wanyakyusa," he politely conceded, "also have schools." Clearly, the woman passenger may not have spoken English, but she certainly understood it.

We passed factories and warehouses surrounded by sturdy masonry fences, car repair shops, and railroad tracks. Signs advertised metal containers, oxyacetylene, furniture, paint, and mineral water. There was a brewery making Tusker Beer, and a bakery from which wafted the delectable smell of baking bread. Dump trucks barreled past, some loaded with standing people. "Taking them to work," our driver explained. Africans walked or bicycled along the roadside or gathered in interested clusters around some focal point of activity, such as a lineman up a telephone pole or a ditch digger. Then, suddenly, there it was, downtown Dar es Salaam, lazing beside a lovely palm-fringed harbor.

Although its newest buildings might have been modern twenty years earlier, and its signs were mostly in English, Dar es Salaam exuded a cosmopolitan air. English cotton dresses, Indian *saris*, boldly-colored African *kangas* and *kitenges*, and voluminous Muslim *buibuis* graced women of three races and several religions. A bronze statue of a native *askari* (soldier), commemorating Africans who had fought for Britain in the First World War, stood in the center of a traffic circle. Automobiles shared the streets with sweating Africans pulling rickshaw-like carts laden with goods. African mamas carried babies in cloth slings on their backs and balanced baskets of fruit on their heads.

Old German colonial government buildings, shaded by coconut palms and cashew trees, stood stolidly along the waterfront and nearby streets. Built before the First World War when Tanganyika was known as German East Africa, they had thick walls, high windows, and wooden shutters. A massive Lutheran church with gothic windows and high spire might have dominated a village in northern Germany. The New Africa Hotel had once been called the Kaiserhof, and looked it. The

Ambulance Corps Band, in crisp white uniforms, was playing spirited marches on the hotel's veranda as we walked by.

We saw small Indian shops with burning incense and gaudy pictures of Hindu gods on the walls, *sari*-clad women with scarlet caste marks on their foreheads, turbaned Sikhs in army and police uniforms. Indians owned many of the commercial establishments and were adept at separating you from your money. A proprietor of a small family clothing shop, seeing one of our group hesitate over a potential purchase, suggested he take the shirt home and wear it first. "You pay me later," he said. Charmed to be so trusted, the volunteer took the shirt and paid on the spot.

We spent the day seeing the sights, eating deep-fried *samosas* and *mandazis,* and looking right instead of left before crossing streets. In the evening we sat by the harbor and watched the gray hulls of anchored freighters turn orange in the sunset. Three- and four-generation families of Indians emerged from the city to walk sedately along the harbor front, enjoying the cooling air. Dusk fell and bats emerged to swoop and jink about in the darkening sky. Then the ships' lights came on, reflecting in silver strands across the water. We roused ourselves and found a taxi back to Mgulani.

With the next day came a surprise: those of us who had expected to be working in southern Tanganyika for the Village Resettlement Program found ourselves being interviewed instead by representatives of another government department.

"Gentlemen, have you really come here just to dig privies?"

We foresters squirmed a little; we hadn't thought of our involvement in quite that light. Two British officers of the Tanganyika Department of Forestry had appeared at Mgulani that morning, politely but firmly requesting a meeting. They wanted us to join their department. We gave them our undivided attention: they were foresters; they were offering us forestry positions; they wore shorts and long socks, into the top of which one man had stuck his pipe. Declaring that we'd be wasted on the Village Resettlement Program, they produced a list of available positions. We had only to choose. Halfway down the list, I saw *Assistant Conservator (Forests) Ngorongoro Conservation Unit*. The Village Resettlement Program lost a volunteer.

The other four volunteers also chose forestry positions. However, none had done as well as I: Not only would I be working at Ngorongoro Crater, which I had expected to visit only once or twice during my stay, but I would also be just next door to the Serengeti National Park. My only regret was that I couldn't see Dad's face when he got my letter.

Now that we knew our postings, it was time to move out of the Salvation Army camp. Many of us were going directly to our places of work: Cathy, the pretty nurse from Philadelphia, had been posted to Mbeya, a small town in the highlands of southern Tanganyika near the Zambia border (unfortunately, about as far from Ngorongoro in northern Tanganyika as it was possible to get). However, those of us with forestry, agriculture, and wildlife jobs still had a week or so of in-country training before taking up our positions. This was to take place at the Tengeru Agricultural School near the town of Arusha, four hundred miles northwest of Dar es Salaam.

Trailed by a swirling cloud of dust, our bus, a snub-nosed blue and white Leyland with a ladder welded to its side, rumbled northward through the dry Tanganyika countryside. At high speeds—the driver's preference, even for corners and bumpy detours—the bus sounded like a cross between a cement mixer and a World War II German Stuka dive bomber. Almost new, it sounded old. Boarding it at the crowded bus station, we handed over our suitcases to be stowed in a large bin on top with the other luggage—cheap fiber suitcases, cardboard boxes tied with twine, bunches of green bananas, foam rubber mattresses—and found our seats in the First Class section, which were so close to a metal partition behind the driver we could barely squeeze into them. We shifted to less-prestigious but more-comfortable seats.

Partial map of Tanganyika showing features mentioned in the book. (1) Lake Natron, (2) Lake Manyara, (3) Mt. Meru. Lake Eyasi (unnumbered) lies west of Lake Manyara.

For much of the way we passed through wooded, gently-undulating country crossed by small muddy rivers. Many trees were leafless. Recent fires had left charred stubble and patches of exposed reddish soil; ashy silhouettes of fallen trees lay where the flames had consumed them. Occasionally, mud-and-wattle huts with thatch roofs appeared by the roadside, as did women walking with children in tow, balancing interesting loads on their heads—a bunch of bananas, a teapot, a bar of soap. Men sat in the shade or sedately pedaled bicycles, some carrying hefty loads, such as a gunny sack of charcoal. I saw an old man using a foot-powered sewing machine.

After a few hours, the bus stopped for a break at a small roadside village, a straggle of small, widely-spaced, mud-plastered huts with thatched or corrugated tin roofs, and a large mango tree shading two old men sitting on wobbly wooden chairs. Women sat flat on the ground, selling mangoes, papayas, and bananas from piles in front of them. Young men hawked fruit and groundnuts through the windows to passengers still on the bus. I had to find a toilet, which meant I had to ask for directions, which meant, I assumed—now that we were some distance from Dar es Salaam—that I must do it in Swahili. Choosing a likely looking man, I mumbled, *"Choo iko wapi?"* (Toilet is where?) I expected him either to gape in incomprehension or split his stomach laughing. Instead, he gave me a big smile, pointed towards the back of a nearby house, and said, "Bwana, you speak good Swahili!" What a relief, I could speak the language after all, or at least one of its more important phrases. There was hope.

That afternoon, the bus traveled along the edge of Maasailand, and the driver stopped several times to pick up members of this tribe of cattle-herding people. Taller, slimmer, and smaller-boned than the other passengers, the Maasai wore a sheet of *Amerikani* cloth knotted at one shoulder, which the men wore to their knees and the women to their ankles. (*Amerikani* cloth was an unbleached calico named after the American traders who introduced it to East Africa.) These robes, or *mashuka*, were rusty-colored from an accumulation of dirt, smoke, and ocher—the latter used to decorate the body—and a minimum of washing. (Washing was a luxury because the Maasai had so little water in their arid environment.) The women's heads were closely shaven and they wore around their necks wide, circular, stiff leather yokes sewn with bright red and white beads. The decorative yokes flapped violently up and down between breast and chin when the women ran, which several had to do to catch the bus.

Invariably, the bus conductor ordered the Maasai to the back of the bus where they, as I understood from the comments of the other Africans, would not offend the eyes and noses of the other passengers: It was a revelation to find, at a time when racism was so much in the news back home, that discriminatory behavior wasn't confined to narrow-minded white people.

Maasai women.

Many of the passengers hadn't fully adapted to the speed of bus travel. Only when the bus was actually rushing past their destination did they rise from their seats and signal that they wanted off. One passenger, a Maasai warrior, speeded his debarkation by giving the post by the door such a violent whack with the flat of his *simi* (short sword) that even the driver, though insulated by the roar and whine of the engine, heard the *whaang* and quickly brought the bus to a slewed stop.

We ended our bus trip at Moshi, a town at the southern foot of Mt. Kilimanjaro. (Moshi in Swahili means smoke.) Young boys swarmed over the bus, grabbed our luggage before we could get to it, and loudly promised to take it wherever we wanted. "Plees, grreeaat serfice sir!" they yelled while trying to out-yank competitors at the other end of the suitcase. But they quickly scattered when a stout British colonial who was waiting to collect us roared, "Get the bloody hell away from those bags you little blankety-blanks"

Our escort drove us to Arusha that night along a blacktopped highway. All around us the bush was burning, distant fires glowing in the darkness like thin molten wires. But the beauty of it was wasted on our host, who saw only blatant transgressions by the *natives*. Laws had been passed against burning, "But just look at how they are obeyed; these people have no discipline!" Implied was an attitude I was to find common among European settlers and civil servants: *Just wait and see what these people do to this country after we go.*

Tengeru Agricultural School was situated at four thousand feet elevation in a lush green landscape of small farms and large coffee plantations. We and some British volunteers were there for purposes of acculturation, which involved Swahili lessons, lectures on appropriate subjects, and field trips. I liked the field trips best. The visit to the Arusha Chini sugar cane estate was especially interesting because of the voluminously baggy khaki shorts worn by our expatriate guide. Standard field issue for the British colonial male, they were very practical for hot, tropical climates. To expedite a flow of cool air around the upper parts of one's legs, they were approximately as wide at the bottom as they were long. Therefore, when in polite company, it was important to wear underpants and watch how you sat down. Our guide wasn't doing either.

Acculturation also occurred in other ways. A good example was early morning tea, which African attendants brought to my tent every morning at 6:30. I was an early riser so it fit right into my routine. I savored cups of sweet, steaming tea while watching rainbow-colored sunbirds flit and hover among the dewy flowers outside my tent. Early morning tea was a cultural accretion that I minded not one bit.

I also learned how to dine properly. Dinner was a several-course affair with coffee taken afterward in another room. Although new to the idea, I did not in the least mind eating many courses; it was the large number of utensils (nine, if I remember correctly) spread around my plate and the social dictum that each be used only for its intended purpose that made life difficult. At first I just used anything that got the job done, but the very correct, white-haired African waiter always replaced my improperly-used utensil with a clean one for the next course. At the end of the meal my poor dining etiquette was marked by several pieces of silver still in front of me while everybody else had bare tablecloth. I caught on fast.

We visited Arusha several times, traveling by *matatus,* commercial minivans that plied the road between Moshi and Arusha. Despite its relatively small population of about ten thousand people, Arusha, for which the almost fifteen thousand-foot-high volcanic cone of Mt. Meru provides a dramatic backdrop, had about everything needed for a civilized existence, including the Metropole movie theater, Twiga Book Store (*twiga* means giraffe), and a theater for amateur plays. Small shops, cafes, residences, and vacant lots, shaded by brightly-flowering jacaranda and flamboyant trees, lined the streets. An old German *boma,* or fort, stood surrounded by tall eucalyptus trees not far from the town's center. Its whitewashed, crenellated, yard-thick walls, pierced by vertical slit windows, recalled a time when the European's control over the land was new and tenuous.

I liked the market with its milling crowd of Africans, many of them Maasai clad in dullish-red *mashuka* and bright beads. Colorful cloths draped the booths. Market women sat on three-legged stools behind piles of tomatoes, Brussels sprouts, and cabbages. There were gunny sacks of charcoal, lengths of sugar cane leaning against stall walls, and clothes laid flat on mats for inspection. And bananas! One could buy yellow bananas, green bananas, and red bananas, incredibly sweet compared to the ones we had at home. There were large bananas and small bananas. There were even cooking bananas that tasted like potatoes—I hadn't realized that so many kinds of bananas existed.

The market was also the place to buy household items, including an unpretentious aluminum cooking pot called *sufuria* (soo-fur-E-a). Found in every household from mud hut to the finest colonial mansion, it came in many sizes and had no handle, only a narrow lip around the top, so that a collection of pots nested neatly one within one another. The very largest *sufuria* could serve as a small wash tub. Lightweight, it was very practical for safari. After many years of living in East Africa, if I were to pick the most iconic of all possible African mementoes, it would be a fire-blackened, dented, scratched *sufuria*.

On to Ngorongoro

After completing training, I visited the Ngorongoro Conservation Unit's office in Arusha to meet with the conservator, Henry Fosbrooke. I wanted to know when to report for work. I hadn't heard from anyone in his organization since signing up in Dar es Salaam, so I wasn't certain he even knew I existed. I located the office, a small two- or three-room affair on a back street, by the logo displayed in its window: a Maasai shield displaying Ngorongoro Crater and an acacia tree flanked by a Maasai warrior and a black-mane lion. Walking in, I interrupted a royal dressing-down of an African clerk by an irate, middle-aged British woman who must have been his boss. Ordering the chastened clerk back to work, she came to the counter.

"Received an advance on his salary a fortnight ago," she complained in a raspy, penetrating voice. "Now he wants a loan even though he hasn't repaid a shilling on the last one. Usually shows up late and continually makes mistakes when he does grace us with his presence. Yes, what do you want?"

Carefully avoiding the topic of the clerk, I introduced myself as the new assistant conservator (forests) and asked to speak with Mr. Fosbrooke, with special reference to when he wanted me to report for duty. "The new AC(F)?" the woman bridled. "I have no such information. Who sent you? The Peace Corps? *American?*" Anyway, I couldn't see Mr. Fosbrooke just now because he was on the phone with someone in the ministry in Dar es Salaam. So, I sat by the window to wait and speculate about my future boss, who must be a strong personality himself to have employed this woman.

Outside, a white settler in shorts, faded green shirt, and safari hat bleached by many washings (for some reason he wore no socks) parked a scratched and dented Land Rover before striding away. I wondered if he was one of the people soon to be dispossessed by the new government without—or so I had heard—any compensation whatever. The government's position was that because Europeans had originally taken the land without asking or paying for it, Africans, now that they were in power, were going to reclaim it the same way. Understandably, the settlers were very bitter. However, short of getting the British government to help the Tanganyikan government buy them out, as it was doing in Kenya, they were powerless.

A beggar sitting cross-legged on the sidewalk looked up hopefully as the settler walked by, but was ignored. He was a small man—almost a dwarf—and hunchbacked, and I was unsure what to make of him because beggars were a new experience for me. For one thing, he seemed so content, with an easy smile and a cheery greeting for passersby, many of whom, apparently used to him, obliged with a coin or two. "Oh don't feel sorry for him," hmmphed the office supervisor, who had come to see what I was looking at. "He's not poor; quite the contrary. He bought a farm with the money he's begged over the years. Wonderful what one can do while sitting on one's backside, isn't it?"

I turned back to the window. Around the corner came a young Indian woman of such stunning loveliness that she should have had a crowd of prospective agents littering her path with acting and modeling contracts. However, this beauty, whose western-style dress proclaimed her a Christian with familial ties to the Portuguese territory of Goa in

India, didn't even have an attendant boy friend. Just as she paused to drop a coin in the beggar's bowl, a minibus, flaunting the distinctive black-and-white zebra stripes of the United Touring Company, suddenly blocked my view. Henry Fosbrooke chose this moment to emerge from his office.

Suddenly there he was beside me, a middle-aged, somewhat portly Englishman with glasses, well-worn woolen sweater vest, and businesslike smile. "Oh, yes, the Peace Corps chap. Pleased to meet you." Then, turning to his formidable office supervisor, he said, "This is Mr. Herlocker who is to be our new assistant conservator (forests). Oh, didn't I inform you about his coming? Well, I wondered why he was so late. No matter: He's here now and ready to go to work—Dennis, you *are* ready to go to work, aren't you? Good! Well, that's that, then. Come, let's go and have some tea. I'm feeling peckish."

Henry escorted me busily down the street towards tea. We passed one café. "The Cha Cha?" he exclaimed, "I never go there. No, I lie. I did go once. The tea was foul and the wretched place has a jukebox. Shall I tell you what it was playing? Elvis Presley. Now really! Come along, we will attend a proper establishment." So off we went to a proper establishment where we sat in the dappled shade of a wide-spreading flamboyant tree (that's actually its name), drank tea, ate those dry cakes that the British so enjoy, and talked about Ngorongoro and my duties there.

I learned that the Ngorongoro Conservation Area (NCA) was three thousand two hundred square miles in area, and comprised the Crater Highlands and the eastern half of the Serengeti Plains. It also included the Northern Highlands Forest Reserve which protected the flora and fauna of the wetter part of the Crater Highlands. The Conservation Area had once been part of the Serengeti National Park from which the Maasai were excluded. But because the Crater Highlands and eastern Serengeti Plains were so important to the Maasai, they were excised in 1959 and made into a multiple-use area administered by the

Conservation Unit. In this way, Ngorongoro Crater was managed as a wildlife preserve; the Northern Highlands Forest Reserve was protected as a source of water for farms along its southern edge; and in certain areas livestock production and agriculture could be supported and regulated. The conservator (Henry) headed everything, and assistant conservators of administration, forests, game, veterinary, and public works answered to him.

My duties were to be numerous. Henry emphasized two of them. First, the forest reserve required protection from illegal grazing by Maasai cattle. Forest guards patrolled it under the supervision of an African forester, but apparently not too well, because many cattle were still getting into the forest. "You must shape these chaps up!" Henry declared. Second, he wanted me to survey and construct roads for tourists to use to view wildlife. "I simply have no one else to do it," he confessed. Then, beaming expectantly across the table at me, added "I'm depending on you now, what?"

Well, this was heady stuff: laying out roads through the African wilderness while herds of game graze in the background and vultures wheel overhead; apprehending spear-bearing warriors in the forest; being trusted and depended upon … I pronounced myself ready to start work. "Excellent," said Henry, putting down his teacup and signaling for the bill, "We go to Ngorongoro tomorrow morning. Be at the office at seven sharp."

I was there at 6:30 a.m. We left at 3:00 in the afternoon. Some unexpected matters had arisen, which Henry needed to attend to on the telephone before leaving (situated a hundred miles to the west, Ngorongoro had no telephone). But leave we eventually did, taking an asphalt road westward across the Maasai Steppe, through open, often rocky grassland with scattered bushes and small thorn trees. We passed herds of livestock tended by small boys, Maasai women following loaded donkeys, and a single rangy warrior walking with long, loping strides, carrying a spear. Grass fires were turning the air hazy with smoke.

Along the way, Henry helpfully named landscape features, pointed out interesting sights, and talked about the Maasai. He explained that the Maasai set grass fires to kill disease-carrying ticks, remove cover that concealed predators, and improve next season's grazing. A pastoral people, they moved about the countryside looking for grass and water for their cattle. Unlike farmers, the Maasai did not want to settle down and send their children to school. Furthermore, although they owned large numbers of livestock, they were not interested in participating in the national economy by selling them. This exasperated the government no end. "Yes, they are an obstinate lot," Henry sighed. At least those were his words; actually, I think he was rather pleased that the Maasai were keeping to their old ways.

At Makuyuni Junction, we turned onto a *murram* road, and soon thereafter came within sight of an imposing escarpment, which Henry identified as the Great Rift. As we approached, we caught glimpses of Lake Manyara, stretching for miles to the south below the escarpment.

At the base of the escarpment, we stopped at a small village called Mto wa Mbu (Stream of the Mosquitoes), where small shops called *dukas* lined both sides of the road; Henry wanted to buy some fresh fruit. Wide-spreading flamboyant trees, some of them in bright scarlet flower, shaded the village. Maasai *murran* wearing sandals cut from old car tires lounged in small groups along the roadside, leaning lightly on their long-bladed spears and looking bored. They carried wooden clubs, and short swords (*simis*) in red leather sheaths, and sported coiffures enhanced with mud and red ocher, which must have taken hours to prepare and maintain. Tourist-filled minibuses passed by on their way to the entrance to Lake Manyara National Park, raising clouds of dust.

We soon set off again. Henry got through his business quickly because he cheerfully paid whatever the merchants asked. "I never bargain!" he explained. From the village, we ascended a thousand feet to the Mbulu Plateau, driving past steaming heaps of fresh elephant dung and loitering troops of baboons who reluctantly yielded way. Henry drove cautiously. Rhinos were common here and had a reputation for charging rather than fleeing when startled. He was driving his personal car that day and didn't want it stove in.

Driving westward across the plateau, we passed scattered fields of golden wheat and the small town of Karatu, which boasted a large Catholic mission. On the roadside, passengers were crowded around a bus, watching their luggage being placed on top; it would be covered with dust when they took it down again. North of the road rose the forested slopes of the Northern Highlands Forest Reserve. It was my first sight of my work area.

Finally, trailing a cloud of red dust, we stopped before an official-looking barrier that marked the entrance to the Ngorongoro Conservation Area. A number of Land Rovers and minibuses were parked by the roadside in front of the barrier. Their drivers were inside the small gate office paying entry fees (the Conservation Area was part of a major tourist circuit through north-central Tanganyika and south-central Kenya). As the dust settled, two green-uniformed gate guards wearing berets marched up to Henry's car and smartly saluted. The conservator had a short conversation with them in Swahili. Then they raised the wooden barrier and we passed through into the Northern Highlands Forest Reserve.

The road climbed. We passed through thickets of broad-leaved shrubs, vines, and creepers that reduced visibility to a few feet except when the road crossed high on the slope and provided us with a view across a small valley. Then we could see widely-scattered trees with smooth silvery bark and dense terminal crowns ascending to heights of up to sixty feet or so. I remarked to Henry that the trees reminded me of marble pillars rising above the overgrown ruins of an ancient city. "You've got it!" he replied. "That's their name—pillar wood."

Eventually we arrived at the top where the road branched both ways along a narrow ridge. Henry stopped and suggested I look over the other side. It took several minutes to absorb the details of that startling view. Expecting a forested valley, I was unprepared to see, far below, tawny grassland stretching away across the floor of an absolutely immense crater. Ngorongoro Crater! All the way through the forest, we had been driving up the crater's southern flank.

The crater's vital statistics—eleven miles wide and two thousand feet deep—are too abstract and dry to describe that view properly. Suffice it to say that the floor of the crater was so deep and wide that it looked empty. Where were the thousands of big game animals for which the crater is famous? Henry had to point them out to me: tiny specks of pepper scattered about the floor. It was indeed a long way down there.

Market at Mtu wa Mbu. Note the gunny sacks of charcoal and banana trees.

We were near our destination now. Late afternoon shadows darkened the western walls of the crater and accentuated small hills on the crater floor. The road kept to the crater rim, passing through grassy glades and dipping into forested gullies. Occasionally, wonderful views presented themselves northward over the darkening crater to the highlands beyond. Then we began to see animals—my first ever free-ranging African wildlife: two gray elephants daydreaming in an open glade, a reddish bushbuck standing startled at the forest edge, the massive black rear of a buffalo disappearing into dense green bush. And finally the best: two lions walking down the middle of the road, so certain of their right of way that, as far as they were concerned, we weren't even there. I started mentally composing my first letter home!

Eventually, we passed the entrance to the Ngorongoro Crater Lodge. Soon after that, Henry turned off onto a smaller road leading past some offices, trucks parked in an open-sided garage, and two tireless Land Rovers resting on blocks. Passing through a low screen of shrubs, we emerged into a large cul-de-sac where four sturdy western-style residences sat enjoying a million dollar view of Ngorongoro Crater. We had arrived.

Getting Started

The First Day

The next morning, which was foggy and wet, Henry took me on an introductory tour, zigzagging down Ngorongoro Crater's southern wall on a narrow road, called the Lerai Track, in a Land Rover. With us were John Goddard, a Canadian biologist, and Tsitote, a Maasai game scout who wore a maroon beret and carried an old British .303 rifle missing most of its bluing. The game scout had wrapped his ear lobes, extended and pendulous from a lifetime of heavy earrings and large ear plugs, over the tops of his ears to keep them out of the way. John had also brought his houseboy along as a treat for him: except for the resident Maasai, Africans seldom had opportunities to visit the crater. The fog had surprised me. Awakening to find it eddying past the window, and hearing condensation from a nearby tree splattering on the corrugated tin roof, I shivered in the moist cold air and wondered if I was in the right place: I hadn't expected to get goose pimples from the cold in Africa. But Henry assured me the fog would stop part way down the crater walls and the crater floor would be sunny and dry, so I stopped worrying about the weather. I was soon to see this famous crater at first hand.

Henry and John had things to do in the crater and at a place called Lemala on the other side, after which we would return by the road along the crater's eastern rim. However, business cropped up earlier than expected for Henry because, halfway down the crater wall, in a narrow swath of forest, we came upon three Maasai men in fog-dampened *mashuka*. They were watering their donkeys and bundling wood they had just cut for transport back down to their *boma* (residence / kraal) on the crater floor.

"This is illegal!" Henry fumed. "Shouldn't be cutting wood here! … rules against it … know it, too … spoke to their *Loibon* [a kind of chief/medicine man] about it last month."

Stopping the car, he said to the Maasai game scout, "Here, Tsitote… tell them …" Then, while Tsitote translated the conservator's message into Maasai, Henry irritably explained to us that most Maasai men understood Swahili well enough but had learned not to show it in the presence of angry officials. The officials, who usually did not speak *Maa*, the language of the Maasai, sometimes just gave up in exasperation and went away. The three men seemed to be following this very strategy because they didn't argue but just stood there looking annoyed. Henry, aware that taking the men into custody would spoil the day's schedule, eventually concluded his harangue and we continued on our way.

Soon the road emerged into sunshine. Now I could see the crater floor, a sea of dry grass enclosing two dark green swamps and a small forest, the latter abutting a wide, tin-colored lake. My companions informed me that Lake Makat was shallow and fluctuated in size depending on the amount of rainfall in the surrounding mountains. The two swamps were called Munge (or Mandusi), and Koitoktok. Lerai Forest was named for its tall, graceful olerai or fever trees (so named because they occur in wet, often malarial areas and were once thought to cause the disease). Swamps and forest alike owed their existence to small streams that flowed into the crater from the surrounding highlands, although Koitoktok also was fed by springs.

Reaching the crater floor we followed a briskly trotting jackal down the road toward Lerai Forest, which Henry wanted to inspect. Cute Thomson's gazelles (Tommies) scattered out of our way; but a high-shouldered kongoni (hartebeest) with long face and lyrelike horns paid us no attention whatsoever.

Leaving the Land Rover, we entered the forest, pushing our way through shoulder-high shrubs. On the way in I discovered that acacia trees have thorns when I stepped on one. It went right through the sole of my tennis shoe; my startled yell flushed birds out of the underbrush. Inside the forest, yellow-barked fever trees seventy feet high radiated a sense of elegance and warmth. Nevertheless, Henry wasn't happy.

"Alas, the reports are true," he said, glumly viewing a fallen fever tree. "They are dying."

Several other fever trees lay nearby, roots exposed, smooth yellow bark gashed and scarred as though they had interacted with heavy equipment on a construction site. Broken branches littered the ground and dangled from standing trees.

Henry stooped to pick up a branch armed with numerous pairs of long white thorns.

"Elephants," he explained. "And a recent rise in the water table, which I suspect is killing the larger trees. I hope we don't lose them all."

I was all ears—this was interesting—but John, who was looking at something in the canopy with his binoculars, wasn't listening. "What *is* that bird up there? Henry, is that a turaco?"

Henry had seen enough, so we left Lerai Forest and drove west into the grassland. For a while we passed among fat-bellied Burchell's zebra grazing peacefully in family groups and eccentric-looking wildebeest, or gnu, with black faces and white beards. The herd sounds engulfed us: wildebeest grunts, *gnuh, gnuh, gnuh*—sounding as undignified as the wildebeest looked—snorts, heavy breathing, softly thudding hooves, and the *rip* of grass being torn from the ground by grazing animals. Sharp barks of zebras punctuated the soft droning. Zebra stallions suddenly nipped, kicked, or, with drumming hooves and bared teeth, chased one another. Elderly looking wildebeests cavorted about as though they had just won the lottery. Or they just stood around doing nothing in particular. It was a peaceful, even idyllic, scene.

But every so often John, Henry, or Tsitote pointed out something of the darker side to life in the crater, such as the dismembered skeleton of a recently killed wildebeest, or a zebra whose tail had been bitten off by hyenas, or a wildebeest whose flanks bore the scars of claws. The herds always kept a respectful distance from passing hyenas, which I learned were the principal predators here, even surpassing lions, which, in the crater, were more likely to scavenge from hyenas than to kill their own food.

Henry showed us some prehistoric graves and called our attention to three deeply worn livestock trails that angled down the western wall of the crater, evidence, he said, that humans had lived here in the distant past, long before the coming of the Maasai. Near a small airstrip, where aircraft with passengers for the Ngorongoro Crater Lodge landed when the upper air strip was fogged in, we came upon a recent kill. It was an eland but there wasn't much of the large antelope left, just some small pieces of gristle on the bones and bits of skin and hair lying scattered about on the ground. Several vultures squatted on the ground nearby, looking grouchy and discontented, as though last night's meal hadn't been up to standard.

From a low hill a few miles north of the lake, we watched herds of wildebeest and zebra in the distance, almost lost in the great immensity of the crater.

"It's a big place," John mused. He handed me his binoculars so I could have a look. "Over twenty-five thousand animals live here but you wouldn't know it, the crater's so large."

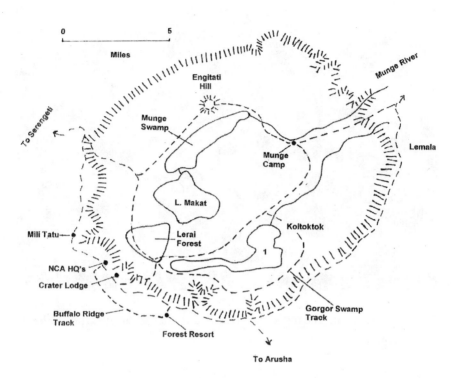

Ngorongoro Crater. (1) Gorgor Swamp.

We could see a tight cluster of tourist vehicles near the edge of Munge Swamp where my colleagues said there probably were some lions, or maybe a rhino; flashes of light heliographed from vehicle windows as they moved about; another car, noticing the activity, hastened over to see what they had found.

"Why don't they stay on the main tracks?" Henry complained. "There's quite enough off-track driving going on. It's wearing down the grass and disfiguring the crater floor. I must talk with our guides about this."

John wasn't pleased either. "Crowding the animals makes them edgy." Then he took his binoculars back.

Maasai *boma*. The dark patches beyond it are old *boma* sites. (Photo by George Frame.)

Below us a herd of Maasai cattle grazed near the Munge River under the watchful eye of their herders. They were from the single Maasai *boma* that remained in Ngorongoro Crater, Henry said. Once there had been more *bomas*, but because the crater was officially devoted to wildlife conservation and tourism, all but one had been removed to reduce the competition between livestock and wildlife for grass. "And," he added, "I soon may be forced to remove that one too." This was because wildlife conservation organizations in Europe and North America, which were providing important financial and moral support to the Ngorongoro Conservation Unit, were incensed about a recent spate of rhino-spearing and were pushing for the complete removal all Maasai from the crater.

At midday, we dropped down the hill, splashed across the Munge River, and moved into the center of the crater again where we came upon Horace, who was a rhino. An extremely lazy rhino, who was sound asleep when we arrived and remained that way for the entire duration of our visit. The only signs of activity from Horace, other than heavy breathing, came from several yellow-beaked tickbirds (ox peckers) that hopped and fluttered about as they poked into nooks and crannies of his body in search of ticks. As there was no opposition from Horace on the matter, we turned off the engine and ate lunch while watching his rib cage rise and fall and the tickbirds feed. There were several deep gashes in his side, a few of which were gently oozing blood. John thought that these were probably old war wounds, perhaps received while battling another rhino, which the constant prodding and pecking of tickbirds kept from healing.

This was my first experience with a rhinoceros outside of a zoo. *This is the fearsome rhinoceros?* Wild rhinos weren't supposed to lie peacefully snoring while strangers sat next to them eating sandwiches; they charged about, putting white hunters up trees and impaling natives on their horns. (I had read up on the subject) However, John, whose principal task here at Ngorongoro was to study rhinos, explained that Horace had not always been easygoing. When the rhino first appeared in Ngorongoro Crater—he was a relative newcomer—he had vigorously charged everything in sight. But now he was so used to daily visits by tourist vehicles that he paid them no attention whatever and just went on with his life, which included lots of sleeping.

"He's an old dear isn't he," Henry enthused. "A perfect photo opportunity for the VIP's I bring to the crater."

"Much good that'll do if a Maasai spears him," John replied. No fan of tourists—VIP's or otherwise—he also distrusted Maasai in the crater as a threat to its rhino population; the sooner that last Maasai *boma* moved out of the crater the better.

Leaving Horace slumbering, we drove to the top of a grassy hill. The day had turned warm and breezy. Soft waves of air swept across the crater floor, bending and flattening the grass as though it was being stroked by an invisible hand. Moving cloud shadows momentarily cooled and darkened the air. Vultures, lifted by newly formed thermals, soared and circled. A party of Indian tourists, equipped with huge telephoto lenses, rolled up beside us but soon spotted something interesting down below. With expectant cries of "tallyho," they bumped their Land Rover down the hill to have a look—at whatever it was. "It's Horace," said John, putting down his binoculars with a grin. "And he's still asleep."

We left the crater via the Munge Track, which ascends the relatively gentle northeastern rim, and entered woodland composed of red thorn acacias. Spur fowl and francolin scratched for seeds and insects along the road. Instead of dodging out of the way, large flocks of guinea fowl raced before us. Only when they were about to disappear beneath the Land Rover's heavy-duty bumper did the noisy birds finally explode into the air with indignant "*kaks*" to land a little way ahead—still on the road—where we soon bore down on them all over again. I thought we would kill some of them but I was wrong. They all eventually escaped into the bushes, still loudly protesting.

Ngorongoro Crater as seen from the Lerai Track. The dark green vegetation on the crater floor is Gorgor Swamp.

Soon after joining the Lemala Road, a dirt track running from Ngorongoro settlement along the eastern rim of Ngorongoro Crater to the tiny hamlet of Nainokanoka, we turned onto a well-used cattle track that headed into the bush. John, who knew little about rhino numbers outside the crater, wanted to look for rhino sign. Fifteen minutes later, Tsitote found it: a bunch of rhino dung.

"Super!" John exclaimed.

"Jolly good! Well done!" Henry enthusiastically concurred.

Both men were worried about rhino poaching, but I was to learn that whereas John focused on the rhino, Henry also worried about the Maasai. He wished them no trouble, as there would be if they were found to be causing a decline in the rhino population. For my part, I was struck by the importance attached to a single pile of manure, which by the way, looks like scattered elephant dung.

"Rhinos begin doing that [kicking apart their dung] when they're about three months old," said John, who then lectured us on some comparative aspects of gender-specific rhino urination behaviors, which I don't need to bother you with here.

Then we stopped to see the game scout at Lemala because Henry and John had some business to discuss with him. His residence was a small wooden hut sitting on a slab of concrete beneath the widespread branches of a large, red thorn acacia tree. The hut was painted green and had a corrugated tin (*mabati*) roof and two unglazed windows with wooden shutters that were closed at night. As we approached, we noticed a cooking fire burning between some rocks. A young woman was just placing a battered-looking *sufuria* over the fire, resting it on the rocks. While the others spoke with the game scout in Swahili—the more-interesting parts being translated by Henry into English so that John could understand—I walked over to see what she was doing

"*Hujambo*," she greeted me, shyly.

"*Sijambo*," I replied. "*Habari gani?*" What is the news?

"*Nzuri.*" Good, she murmured politely, keeping her eyes lowered; "*Karibu.*" Welcome.

"*Asante.*" Thank you. "*Unafanya nini?*" What are you doing?

"*Na tengeneza chai.*" I am making tea, she said, as she poured a large container of milk into the *sufuria* and began stirring it with a long-handled wooden spoon.

Our conversation ended at this point because she was shy and I was out of words. She quietly continued stirring the milk while I searched about for something to say in Swahili. Once the milk began to boil, the woman poured loose tea from a small green package labeled *Simba Chai,* or Lion's Tea, into the pot, stirred the darkened mixture a while longer, and then removed the pot from the fire. Pouring its contents into several large fist-sized, enameled tin cups, she turned and called out, "*Karibu chai.*" Come have some tea.

I had never seen tea like this. At the time, Americans drank even less tea than they do now, so I wasn't an expert on the subject. Nonetheless, I couldn't help thinking that this lady had not put milk in her tea she had put tea in her milk.

By this time Henry and John had finished their business with the game scout and walked over to join me. Ignoring the cups of steaming tea sitting on the concrete slab, they talked about what they had learned. The good news was that Martin, the game scout, had confirmed the presence of a male rhino in the area and had also seen a female between here and Nainokanoka, several miles to the north. However, when asked about the situation farther to the east on the southern slopes of Lolmalasin Mountain, the game scout had been evasive.

"I bet he hasn't even been there," John complained. "Can't be bothered to get off his duff and walk a bit. Henry, these game scouts need more supervision."

"Precisely," Henry agreed. "But I can do little until the Game Department seconds me another assistant conservator (game), one they don't just want to get rid of. It would also help if the ministry gave me enough funds to …"

Now, this sounded interesting. Here was a chance to learn about behind-the-scenes happenings within the Conservation Unit. Who, for instance, had been the last assistant conservator (game) and why had he left? I was all ears as I absent-mindedly picked up one of the cups of tea. Then I abruptly dropped it and danced about for a while flapping my fingers in the air.

"Pole sana!" exclaimed the woman, with startled eyes *"Chai ni moto sana!"* That's very hot tea! (Thereby confirming my suspicions.)

"Mmm, yes, tin cups. Good conductors of heat you know," commented Henry.

"Best to let tin cups cool a little before you pick them up," added John helpfully.

The two of them then talked for several more minutes about needed improvements and funding before they reached over to pick up their cups. I hesitantly followed suit, using my unburned hand this time, and took a sip. And, sure enough, it tasted like hot milk with tea in it. But it also tasted smoky—very smoky. "Why's this taste so smoky?" I asked my mentors. "It's the milk," Henry answered. "The game scout's wife buys it from the Maasai who carry it in gourds which they clean afterward by upending over a smoky fire. The milk soaks up the smoky taste from the gourds."

"They also clean the gourds with piss," added John.

Piss?

"Hupendi chai?" asked the game scout's wife, bringing me out of my reverie.

"She's asking if you dislike the tea," translated Henry.

"Ah, well … no, it's, ah, fine," I managed to say.

"Well, better drink it down, then, because it's getting late and we should be on our way."

I grudgingly followed instructions and we headed home, driving southward a few miles along the eastern rim of Ngorongoro Crater before stopping to look at a small herd of elephants. Actually we had no choice in the matter because one of them was in the center of the road. We watched as the big animals unhurriedly foraged about in the bushes and trees or just stood quietly meditating.

"I say, John, that one looks familiar."

John studied the elephant with his binoculars. "Yes—that broken tusk. But where—"

"By Jove, I have it!" Henry suddenly exclaimed. "Lake Manyara! It was standing near the park gate the last time I was there. You know what this means don't you? It proves my theory that elephants move between Manyara and Ngorongoro and that I'm right in wanting to protect a corridor for wildlife movements between the Park and Conservation Area. The Minister must be informed as soon as possible. Well, I *am* chuffed about this!" Just then, the elephant standing on the road gave a great whoosh of a sigh and ambled off the road far enough to allow us to continue our journey.

However, hardly a mile or so later, Henry stopped again and excitedly pointed out the window. "Dennis, see those cattle? They're in the forest reserve." Sure enough, several hundred feet away to the south of the road, a herd of cattle, accompanied by several Maasai *murran*, was disappearing into a stand of large shrubs.

Exasperated, Henry declared, "We really must do something about this trespassing." Turning to me in the back seat he added, "Even when we let them graze the glades during droughts, the herders don't stay there but take their livestock right inside the forest. And they *will* set fires."

"And spear rhinos," added John, grimly.

But making an arrest meant that we would have to trek the cattle to Ngorongoro, which required more people and time than we had. So, we continued on.

Fresh cowpats on the road indicated the recent passage of another herd of bovines, either Maasai cattle or buffalo. Our speculations as to which ended when, near the junction with the main road from Arusha, we found a herd of thirty-some buffaloes grazing in a roadside glade. Black, muscular animals with massive, up-curled horns like the wings on an airborne soldier's badge, they were roughly the size of cattle, although more powerful—and meaner—looking. (Actually, they looked like a bunch of thugs.) Heads up, they regarded us alertly.

Suddenly Peter, John's houseboy, broke into speech. "*Nyati!*" he hissed. Buffalo. "Buffalo are very bad! Very! *Nyati mbaya sana! Sana!*" A torrent of passionate Swahili followed, which surprised us because so far Peter had been relatively quiet. Henry translated: "He says that many buffalo lived near his village. They broke fences, and trampled crops. Sometimes they killed people who encountered them unexpectedly. He warns us to be very wary of them."

Consequently, when several of the big black beasts detached themselves from the herd and advanced on us at a heavy trot, my interest sharpened. Was this a charge? But then halfway to the car, they stopped. They were a rough-looking bunch: their eyes were runny; cakes of dried mud adhered to their flanks; one had a split nostril and a long line of drool dripping from its muzzle. "It's been fighting something," said John. The buffalo maintained their watchful stance for a few minutes, occasionally shaking their heads to dislodge pesky tickbirds. Then, with explosive snorts, they suddenly wheeled and lumbered back to the herd which fled, rumbling noisily before them into the forest.

Soon afterward, we offered a ride to three dusty Wambulu men walking towards Ngorongoro. They wore well-used, Western-style clothes and one of them had a small bundle tied to a staff that he carried over his shoulder. "Probably looking for work, either with us or the lodge," Henry had said. "We'd best pick them up for there's no telling what they may meet on the road between here and Ngorongoro."

Salutations flew back and forth as the men climbed in: "*Hujambo—sijambo—habari gani—nzuri—karibu*;" they were happy to get the ride, doubly so when later on we rounded a corner and found four lions resting in the middle of the road.

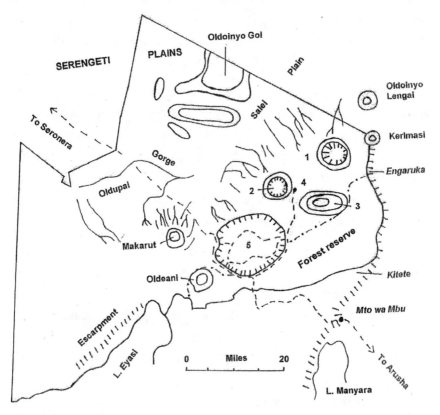

Map of the Ngorongoro Conservation Area showing the Crater Highlands in the east and the Serengeti Plains in the west. (1) Empakaai Crater, (2) Olmoti Crater, (3) Lolmalasin Mountain, (4) Nainokanoka Village, (5) Ngorongoro Crater.

Back at the settlement we got out and stretched as Peter, resuming his job as houseboy, began unloading firewood we had found along the way. At the invitation of Mrs. Goddard we would be eating together tonight, so after cleaning up, I sat outside and watched the advance of evening dim the features of the crater and the highland peaks beyond. A shaggy-haired waterbuck with long horns that curved back and up, watched me for a few minutes before moving away. A small bat fluttered spookily about—actually more felt than seen—chasing insects in the dusk. A sudden *whish* came from a shrub-choked gully, the sound of a large animal expelling its breath. Night birds began to call. Then I heard African voices in lively discussion somewhere behind me, among them Peter's, his speech liberally sprinkled with "*nyatis*" and "*mbaya sanas*" booming with the assurance of having a good tale to tell.

It had been quite a day.

Finally to Work

On my second day at Ngorongoro I learned that my duties included overseeing the Northern Highlands Forest Reserve, ten forest guards, a tiny tree nursery, and a plantation of eucalyptus trees planted to provide fuel for the settlement. The most pressing problem within the forest was Maasai cattle trespassing along the northern border about twenty miles away. But the conservator wanted me to do other things as well, such as locating new game-viewing tracks for tourists. This received the enthusiastic backing of my next-in-command, Mr. Mlangai, a soft-spoken African forester who had been running the tree nursery and plantation very well without me and wanted to continue doing so.

Well, it mattered little to me. I was young and motivated, and only had two years to accomplish anything, and a significant part of that was already being wasted by this idle chatter in the office—two years seemed a pretty short time just then. However, my proposal to start clearing the forest of trespassers tomorrow was quickly shot down: It was the middle of the month and my official Land Rover had already finished its monthly fuel allotment. My colleagues' expressions betrayed astonishment that even a greenhorn could expect a petrol (gasoline) ration to last past mid-month.

"So then, let's start that new tourist track you want to build," I suggested to the conservator. He nixed that one too. "Umm … well, I'm afraid that won't be possible either," he said. "I haven't borrowed the bulldozer for that job from the Public Works Department in Arusha yet."

A quick glance at Mr. Mlangai brought an instant response: "Ah, Mr. Dinnis, the trees nursery has no problems please, and no *tembo* (elephant) in the trees plantation for three weeks now!" In the end, I had to spend the next few days in my office going through the correspondence and reports of my predecessors.

As mist eddied about outside the window and seeped in through a large knothole in the wall, I sat down at a solid-looking desk backed by a wall poster exhorting people to plant more trees. Selecting the topmost file from a stack on the desk, I started reading. Arranged in chronological order were requests from managers of the coffee estates along the southern edge of the forest reserve to cut poles, letters from the Regional Forester about demarcating the forest reserve boundary, price lists for forest produce, and so forth. A red string attached to the back of each file cover held the files—typed letters, mimeographed reports, hand-written notes—in place. The reports contained odd-sounding British forestry terms—*withes, coupes, girth, pricking out*, etc.—which I probably would have to learn. The standard complimentary close to all official correspondence was the very formal, "*I Remain, Sir, Your Obedient Servant.*" I learned right away it was not to be taken literally. It appeared everywhere, even on a letter of resignation in which the officer denounced his boss, Henry, as being of such low moral character that he could no longer work with him.

Scattered through the files were technical reports that gave a picture of the forestry situation in Tanganyika. For a tropical country, it had surprisingly little rain forest. Most of its forest estate consisted of *miombo* woodlands where dry seasons were long, grass fires frequent, and tsetse flies abundant. Moreover, the principal tree of economic value, Mninga, grew so slowly that in order to ensure a sustained yield, only one tree per square mile could be cut each year. Thus, the Forest Department planned to provide the bulk of country's future wood needs from plantations of fast-growing exotic softwood conifer species, primarily Monterey and Mexican pines. They were to be established in high altitude grasslands in the Southern Highlands. Tanganyika's most productive natural forests—closed high forests (tall trees with a closed canopy)—were limited in area (three thousand six hundred square miles). Occurring on widely scattered mountains, they were valued as much for their role in watershed protection as for their tree species such as red mahogany, East African camphorwood, Mvule, and Loliondo. The latter were exploited for their high quality wood used for making, among other things, cabinets and furniture.

Wedged between a bulky Manila file cover and a lurid green one with a bright scarlet diagonal band marked *Secret* (disappointingly, it held no secrets at all), the official management plan for the Northern Highlands Forest Reserve—twenty-six mimeographed foolscap pages bound in a stiff blue cover—was so thin that I almost missed it. According to it, the forty-four by eight-mile reserve dated from 1914, during the German colonial administration, and protected closed high forest that had been degraded by fire and livestock. Although the plan allowed for local exploitation of honey, timber, poles, fuel wood, and grazing, the principal purpose of the reserve was to protect the water catchments and wildlife habitat on the outer southern and eastern slopes of the Crater Highlands. Thus, the major management activities were controlling grazing and fires. Having discovered the limitations imposed by my vehicle's fuel ration, I wondered how successful I would be at doing either one.

"Dennis, I've a job for you!" I was engrossed in a report by an earlier AC(F) on how barbed wire fencing had failed to protect Ngorongoro's small tree plantation from the depredations of wildlife. Duikers oozed through the fence like amoebas; bushbuck, he suspected, jumped over it; buffalo and rhino broke through the wire; and elephant just grabbed the posts and pulled the fences over. I had reached the point where the writer was recommending upgrading to an electrified fence (from his tone he probably would have preferred landmines) when these most welcome words broke through.

Henry had remembered several boxes of meteorological equipment purchased for the construction of a weather station. Now, rescued from the storehouse, they sat on his office floor. "Dennis, this weather station wasn't built, because, until you came, we had nobody who could do it."

I found a spot behind the office that was free of abandoned equipment, and fenced it. Then I assembled the weather station. This consisted of a wooden box with louvered sides (to be set about four feet off the ground), and instruments for recording temperature, humidity, wind speed and direction, solar radiation, and hours of sunshine. The latter instrument, a solarimeter, was a six-inch-diameter crystal ball of the fortune-telling type, which, in concentrating the sun's rays, burnt a narrow path along a strip of heavy paper, graduated in hours. That is, it did once the solarimeter was precisely positioned: it took me a week to get it to where the thin, burnt path continued along the exact middle of the paper strip instead of careering off the side sometime about noon. From then on, the crystal ball on its pillar lent a slightly magical aura to the weather station. It also probably confirmed some people's beliefs about how weathermen predict the weather.

"Well done!" Henry exclaimed. "Now you can take over our rain gauge system." He pushed a cardboard box across the desk at me. It contained a pile of data collection forms, some of which had been filled in, and a glass cylinder graduated in inches and millimeters. Several dead bugs lay at the bottom of the cylinder. "The *boffins* (scientists /

experts) at the East African Meteorological Department at Muguga [near Nairobi, Kenya] have queried some rainfall data we sent them. Our people doing the recording are probably making mistakes. Be a good chap and clear it up, won't you?"

I carried the box back to my little office on the other side of the courtyard where a morning's perusal of records revealed eight sites within the Ngorongoro Conservation Area where rainfall was recorded daily, and a further four rain gauges in the crater that apparently were recorded whenever anyone got around to it. One site showed ten inches of rain in a single day where daily rainfall seldom exceeded a few tenths of an inch. Another site showed no rain at all during two successive rainy seasons. Some sites showed more gaps than data.

Further investigation was clearly needed. This began the next morning when I accompanied the office clerk, who was the designated meteorological observer for this site, on his morning visit to the office rain gauge. It was a bright and sunny, absolutely beautiful, day. The morning air was refreshingly cool and the grass was still wet with yesterday's rain. To the north, the flat-looking summit of Olmoti Mountain (which actually had a large crater inside) stood out like an etching in the crystalline, rain-cleansed air. Yes, I thought, it was a wonderful day to be reading rain gauges—or doing just about anything else for that matter. The clerk, obviously from some warmer part of the country, may not have shared this opinion because he was wearing a heavy, long- sleeved woolen sweater and gum boots.

The rain gauge consisted of a metal container about two feet deep and maybe six inches wide with a funnel at the top that collected the rainwater and directed it into a small metal bucket inside. I watched as the clerk removed the funnel, lifted out the bucket, and poured the rainwater it contained into a glass measuring cylinder like the one I had been given. Then I peered over his shoulder as he lifted the glass cylinder to eye level and made the reading.

"See?" he said. "It is 0.05 of an inch."

"Yes, I see. By the way, where's the recording form?"

"It's in the office, sir." (I had attained "sir" status. I liked that.)

"Okay, after you have entered today's rainfall bring me the form will you?"

He did. I checked the form. Today's rainfall had been entered as 0.5 inches. Yes, that explained a lot.

However, that was just the tip of this iceberg of a problem. For instance, Maasai herders took the small metal buckets inside the gauges to use as milk and water containers. The buckets were replaced with those ubiquitous items of East African glassware, beer bottles. But they quickly overflowed during downpours, which happen quite a lot in East Africa. Accumulations of dead beetles or flying termites frequently blocked the funnels, resulting in under measured rainfall. Most of the glass measuring cylinders eventually broke and often were not replaced for some time because of logistical and bureaucratic delays. The observers, often teachers at rural schools, were frequently absent: sick with malaria, away buying supplies, or on vacation. Some observers did not realize that continuous day-by-day recordings were necessary. In Ngorongoro Crater, hyenas were the problem. Rain gauges seemed to attract them. As hyenas have jaws and teeth of bone-crushing strength, this not only resulted in dented and twisted metal but also in some of the gauges' being yanked right out of the ground.

But these problems could be fixed. We just had to replace broken equipment, and train and monitor the observers better. Additional funds were needed and my Land Rover's monthly fuel allotment would have to be increased, but I was certain that the conservator would agree to both once I explained the situation.

One foggy morning as we walked up the driveway from our houses to the office, Henry striding purposefully along, his body tilted forward as if unhappy with the slow pace of his feet, hugging a thick file (NCA 7/461—Water Supply) to his chest, I proposed my solution.

"Good," he declared. "See to—oh my, look at that." He pointed toward a small stand of eucalyptus saplings planted when foresters still thought barbed wire fences could keep wild animals out. "The buffalo have girdled another tree." Sure enough, one of the twenty-foot trees flaunted a ragged belt of bright cambium where a buffalo had rubbed away the bark with its horns. The tree would now die, as a number of others in the stand had already done. "We must do something about this, Dennis. What do you suggest?"

"Ahhh—"

"Hi! You, there, Edward! What are you doing?" Henry suddenly yelled, waving down the driver of a passing Land Rover. "You should be gathering fuel wood at Endebess today."

"Sir, Mr. Shah [the accountant] wants me to take him to Arusha,"

"Did you tell him that I had arranged for you to do something else?"

Silence.

"You didn't, did you? Why not?"

More silence.

Henry gritted his teeth and said, "Get yourself to Endebess immediately. Bring the wood to me before you dump it so that I may inspect it. Mr. Shah can go to Arusha some other time." As the driver hurriedly drove away, Henry turned back to me, shaking his head, but saying nothing further on the subject of Edward.

"Now, about these buffalo getting into the compound at night, I've decided to—oh drat!" he interrupted himself again, having noticed several Maasai elders waiting outside his office door. "There's that old rogue Serenika and his cronies. They probably want a vehicle and driver to take them to Loliondo—that's a full day's drive from here, you know—to meet with the District Officer and it will take me all morning to convince them that it just isn't on. I have an important meeting with the Regional Engineer, too."

"Henry, you were saying—"

"Ah, I have it," Henry exclaimed, "Solomon, my next-in-line. He speaks Maasai and thinks he knows everything. I will put him onto Serenika. That will get both of them off my back for a while. Yes, that will work very well indeed," he gloated before changing topics again. "By the way, Dennis, Mlangai, that forester chap of yours, is late with his tree planting report. Please remind him. He hates to write, you see; won't do it at all unless he's forced to."

By this time we were at Henry's office door. He greeted *Mzee* Serenika (*mzee*, a mark of respect, means old man) and sent a messenger off to find Solomon. His secretary informed him that the Regional Engineer awaited within and the manager of the Ngorongoro Crater Lodge and several other people of varying degrees of importance wanted a word with him at his earliest convenience.

"Dennis, those recommendations of yours," he said. "See to them will you?"

"And the additional funds and fuel?" I prompted.

"Additional …?" he repeated as though this was the first he had heard about it. "Alas, I'm afraid that is out of the question. The money simply is not there. Furthermore—you were to be officially notified of this tomorrow but I might as well tell you now—the ministry has reduced next month's fuel allotment by half, so your vehicle's allotment has been adjusted accordingly." Then, he considered me thoughtfully for a few seconds.

"Know anything about water supply systems?"

"Ah …," I seemed to be saying this a lot today. "No, I'm afraid not."

"Pity."

With that, he disappeared into his office, leaving me in the cold, drippy fog with additional meteorological duties, unchanged finances, and reduced fuel allowance. However, I'd managed to escape involvement with the water supply system. That was something.

Colleagues, Elephants, and Game-viewing Tracks

The Conservators

Henry Fosbrooke fit my stereotype of a headmaster of a British public school: a mixture of harried, perhaps not-too-efficient administrator, professional instructor, and opportunistic public relations man. But he was a passionate conservationist. Having spent nearly thirty years as a district officer and anthropologist in the Tanganyika territorial government, several of them in Maasailand, and having served on the select committee that created the Ngorongoro Conservation Area, he was the obvious person to be the first conservator.

His colleagues sometimes found him difficult to work with. Indeed, the Conservation Unit did experience a high turnover of officers seconded from other government agencies. However, it was not entirely Henry's fault. Most of his assistant conservators had two bosses: their departmental heads back in Dar es Salaam or Arusha, who continued to pay their salaries and promote or demote them, and Henry, who did neither. Naturally the officers usually identified with, say, the Department of Forestry, or the Department of Game, rather than the Ngorongoro Conservation Unit. But Henry's manner didn't help. He had strong opinions and no compunction about expressing them. His personality frequently grated, and he often "interfered."

At least that was the view of John Goddard, whom Henry often attempted to involve in duties outside his official terms of employment. John handled these situations by going on safari and not returning until Henry returned to Arusha and couldn't get at him any more.

Henry was devoted to his work, especially to the public relations side of it. An enthusiastic publicist of Ngorongoro Crater, he arranged tours by distinguished personalities during which convoys of Land Rovers containing celebrity, entourage, and Henry would zigzag across the crater floor from lion pride to hyena dens to sleeping rhino, with Henry determinedly smiling, lecturing, directing, and photographing all the way. He had a tendency to drop names ("Prince Bernhard and I agree that ..."), but Henry never forgot what he was working for. A rich oilman, shocked by Henry's account of the recent spearing of a rhino by the Maasai, might provide money for a new vehicle for the game scouts. A royal prince of a nation providing foreign aid to Tanganyika might agree to speak with his excellency, the president, about the government's "unfortunate" decision to reduce the Ngorongoro Conservation Unit's budget.

Unfortunately, experience, commitment, and contacts with influential foreigners were not enough to save Henry's job. I had not been at Ngorongoro very long before he met the fate that awaited every expatriate government officer in the country: the government *Africanized* his position. Henry might have kept his job by becoming a citizen of Tanganyika, as a few Europeans had done, but I seriously doubt it. Someone else wanted the job and Henry belonged to the wrong "tribe." He had to go. Henry, thinking the government ungrateful for his many years of labor on its behalf, was hurt. He had not really expected to be replaced for a long time, if ever. I was to see the posts of several of these old expatriate government officers *Africanized* over the next few years, and all of these public servants felt betrayed even when they were properly treated. They really thought the Africans needed them and wanted them to stay. The perceptual gap between expatriate and African obviously yawned wide and deep.

Many colonial officers had the additional problem that there was no future for them back in Britain, either. They had remarkable skills. However, their ability to live in the bush, pack a Land Rover properly for safari, speak native languages, cull dangerous wildlife with a big rifle, or spend weeks walking beside a loaded camel to administer a district the size of Switzerland didn't count for much back home. Besides, it was so rainy and drab and small back there.

Luckily, Henry didn't have to go back. Old enough to retire and with the funds to do it, he stayed in Tanganyika. His retirement home, perched on the lip of a small, lake-filled volcanic crater near Arusha, enjoyed a view that included the lake set within steep, densely forested crater walls, and in the distance, the vast Maasai Steppe. The house was the epitome of English country cottages with its small lush lawn, densely foliaged arbors, brick pathways, and brilliant flowered shrubs; inside were cool shadows, dark paneled walls, small-paned leaded bow windows, cushioned chairs, and deferential servants. Who could blame him for staying?

Solomon ole Saibull, who replaced Henry as conservator, was thirty-some years old. Stocky of build, he had a high-pitched voice and an incipient potbelly. He considered himself a Maasai—ole means "son of" in Maasai—and, as he was the correct age, also a Maasai warrior. He didn't look it. Classic Maasai warriors were tall, slender, and athletic; sported fancy mud hairdos; rubbed red ocher on their skin; carried long nasty-looking spears; and when they were not off somewhere rustling cattle, stood around looking arrogantly bored. Solomon had no problem being arrogant, but he completely failed to be tall, slender, and athletic. Furthermore, he was not strictly a Maasai but rather a member of the Warusha tribe, a *Maa*-speaking group of people living

Henry Fosbrooke and Mr. Mlangai discussing the Ngorongoro Conservation Unit's plantation of fast-growing eucalyptus trees.

near Arusha on the slopes of Mt. Meru. Although linguistically and culturally Maasai, the Warusha farmed, and everyone knew that *real* Maasai didn't farm: They herded cattle and "liberated" them from other tribes—or married Warusha women who did the farming for them. However, Solomon refused to accept that this made a particle of difference. He was, he insisted, Maasai.

A strong-willed person, Solomon was an effective conservator, even when dealing with his *Maa*-speaking kinsmen. If anything, he was firmer with them than his predecessor had been. He needed to be tough because, in addition to the problems generated by the Maasai and Warusha, he also inherited many others. One was the tendency of some junior staff to misappropriate public funds and materials. During my stay with the Ngorongoro Conservation Unit several of its junior employees were jailed for theft, even Abdi (or so we will call him). Abdi was a mechanic who had been with the Unit for several years, and was one of the few nonlocal Africans who actually liked the cool temperatures and damp fogs of Ngorongoro. Because he was personable, had been around long enough to become the Conservation Unit's institutional memory, and kept everything working, Abdi was a valuable employee. However, one day, acting on an anonymous tip, Solomon caught him with a house full of stolen government equipment. Abdi spent the next few years in prison.

At least one set of guards manning the entry gate to the Ngorongoro Conservation Area was caught stealing tourist entry fees every year I was there. I would have found the situation depressing had I been the conservator, but it didn't bother Solomon, who seemed stimulated by crises and spirited disagreements. They kept his juices flowing and relieved the tedium of his administrative duties. After every arrest, he called in his senior officers and, with great relish, demonstrated the most recent way in which his protective accounting measures had been circumvented. (Miscreants who escaped discovery for longer than usual were regarded as especially worthy opponents.) Then, having sent the latest bunch of wrongdoers off to court, Solomon enthusiastically thought up new protective measures and hired another set of gate guards (and, as it usually turned out, future jailbirds).

Although I usually rubbed along smoothly with both of the conservators, Solomon and I did have occasional heated disagreements which, due to the differences in our temperaments and official positions, I usually lost. Getting angry always put me in a foul mood for days afterward, even when I won the argument, but it never seemed to bother Solomon in the least. Indeed, he rather looked forward to having a good tussle and seldom took it personally when I became angry. For instance, not long after I had had an especially rancorous meeting with him, during which I actually pounded on his desk, he called me into his office and, instead of giving me twenty-four hours to pack up and leave, asked if I would stay on another year.

Anthony Mgina, the senior assistant conservator of the Ngorongoro

Conservation Unit under both Fosbrooke and Solomon ole Saibull, was in his late fifties. A short man with big round spectacles and a serious disposition, he was a conscientious and capable administrator who had been posted all over the country by the colonial (or more precisely, territorial) administration. Promoted to positions of increasing responsibility, he eventually achieved the sort of staff sergeant-type position that kept the wheels of so many government departments turning. Anthony had an ability to deal with recalcitrant laborers, irritated tourists, absent-minded superiors, and overbearing ministers that bore no resemblance to his short stature.

Nonetheless, Anthony spent the entire time I was there trying to retire. He wanted nothing more than to return to his tribal home in the southern part of the country, two or three days away by bus. He yearned to work his small farm plot, bounce his grandchildren on his knee, and sit in the shade with other old men. However, his superiors in the ministry wouldn't let him because they couldn't find a qualified Tanganyikan to take his place. (Tanganyikans were only beginning to be trained to replace the British expatriate officers in the administration.) Unfortunately for Anthony, the government expected him to soldier on as a "Nation Builder" until someone was found to replace him. Nonetheless, Anthony persisted in trying to retire. Every few months he drove to Arusha to resubmit his petition, then returned a few days later to resume his duties and wait for the ministry's reply, which was invariably *No*. Anthony was still in harness when I left Ngorongoro. A few years later, when Solomon ole Saibull resigned to return to Dar es Salaam, Anthony was promoted to the position of conservator. Now he was boss, poor guy.

The Buffalo Ridge Track

Late one afternoon, a lowboy truck carrying a D-4 Caterpillar tractor, its driver, and his assistant (referred to as the *turnboy*) eased its way into the Conservation Unit's compound; Henry's request for assistance from the Public Works Department in Arusha had been granted. It was time to put in a new game-viewing track for tourists.

The following day Henry drove me in his Land Rover into the bush behind the settlement to where several acres of native vegetation had been cleared for a fuel-wood plantation of fast-growing eucalyptus trees. An electric fence protected the plantation from wildlife. Where the track ended at a twenty-foot wall of dense bamboo thicket, Henry gave me his instructions. They were simple enough: I was to extend the track eastward to the Forest Resort run by Mr. Dhillon Singh three or four miles away. It would connect with the main road along the crater rim to create a game-viewing circuit from which tourists could see wildlife in a forested setting. Besides the bulldozer and its small crew, I was to have four laborers.

That was okay with me. All I needed was a map and compass.

"Henry, where can I get a map of this area?"

"Sorry, there are none. They don't exist."

"How about a compass?"

"Oh dear, we don't have any. Remind me to order one will you?"

The next day, unencumbered by map or compass, the forest officer, Mr. Mlangai, and the rest of us pushed into the dense bamboo and headed in what I hoped was an eastward direction to reconnoiter the route. That Mr. Mlangai was along only as an interested spectator was deducible from his clean, white, short-sleeved shirt, street shoes, and fedora hat; tomorrow he would return to growing and planting trees, which he felt were a forester's *proper* duties. In contrast, the laborers—called *day laborers* because they were hired on that basis—wore dirty wrinkled clothes, and footwear of gum boots, rubber tire sandals, or bare feet. A Maasai wore the usual toga-like *Amerikani* cloth that once had been white but was now a dirty reddish brown. Scrapes and scratches gleamed whitely against the black skin of his bare legs.

We were lucky we didn't get lost because, about three hours later, we found we'd missed the Forest Resort by about a quarter of a mile. With relief we spotted it at the far end of a large open glade, a several-room brick structure with four chimneys and a verandah fronting a large gully. However, the area we had passed through had been both attractive and interesting. The topography was gentle, which made for easy road building, and the landscape was intriguingly exotic. Dense thickets of light green bamboo mixed with stands of tall, dark-leaved pillar wood trees looked more like old China than Africa. Wisps of lichen and delicate white orchids hung from tree branches. Sun-filled glades of tall manyatta grass edged with yellow-flowering crotalaria shrubs punctuated the dimness and shadows of the forest and frothy-topped bamboo thicket. Although empty at the time, the glades seemed made to order as a backdrop for herds of grazing buffalo and elephant.

We saw no animals that day although I almost stepped on one—gave me quite a start. Suddenly there was an explosion right at my feet followed by a ripple of grass streaking rapidly across the glade and into the bamboo thicket on the far side. We never saw the animal, just the grass moving, but the experience made my pulse race for a minute or two. Mr. Mlangai said we were lucky this was the *only* animal we had encountered. He was probably right, too, because there was plenty of animal sign about, including piles of buffalo and elephant dung, tree trunks worn smooth by the rubbing of large bodies, trails forced through the dense bamboo, and mud wallows, one directly across a small stream from the Forest Resort. Henry was probably right about its being a good place for viewing game.

The following morning we made our way again into the dense bamboo, this time to begin marking the route of the new track. Behind us we could hear the approaching *clank, clank, clank* of the D-4 Caterpillar tractor "walking" its way up the old track from the settlement. Not long thereafter, guided by the narrow trail we were cutting, the bulldozer roared its way into the thicket.

I planned to mark enough track to keep the caterpillar busy for a few hours and then plunge ahead to scout the next section. But as Mr. Mlangai had warned, we began encountering wildlife. Within minutes we surprised a large herd of buffalo, which moved only a short distance away. They stayed close by, glowering at us the rest of the morning despite the racket made by the tractor. This kept us from getting too far ahead of the bulldozer.

The next morning we hadn't even reached our starting point yet when we ran into elephants feeding along the edge of the fuel-wood plantation. Crossing into the plantation to put the electric fence between them and us, we yelled and whistled until the elephants disappeared into the bamboo.

The third day began with a welcome absence of big animals, so I resurrected my plan to scout ahead of the tractor. I climbed a nearby tree to look out over the tops of the bamboo and see what lay ahead (grassland, I hoped). The answer was lots more bamboo. So I climbed down again to where my crew were psyching themselves up for the day's work with a rousing rendition of the TANU song (the Tanganyika African National Union was Tanganyika's ruling political party), and resignedly set out.

I soon learned that the troops were not happy to be in the bush with nothing to fend off dangerous beasties but a few blunt *pangas* (machetes) and some ten-foot lengths of bamboo stakes. The Maasai laborer, who I assume would not have been as bothered, had left us for the time being. Calling me *Bwana Miti*, or Mr. Trees, the Swahili term for forester, they cautioned me to move slowly (*polepole*) and watch out for elephant (*tembo*) and buffalo (*nyati*). One of them also kept warning me about *mbogo*, which I took to mean *mboga*, or vegetables. As I didn't feel in any immediate danger from thundering herds of vegetables, and showed it, he became increasingly anxious and voluble until one of the other laborers, who knew some English, clued me in: *mbogo* is another name for buffalo.

We pressed onward, Bwana keeping up appearances by *acting* unconcerned about buffalo or elephant. For some time we threaded our way cautiously through the bamboo. At one point I glimpsed a buffalo walking away from us as I turned a corner of a narrow trail; I waited for him to disappear before continuing. Another time we heard elephants breaking branches off to one side of us. We could also hear their stomachs rumbling, so they must have been very near.

Eventually we emerged from the cool dimness of the bamboo into a grassy glade, where it was sunny and an occasional light breeze stirred the grass. For a while we waded through waist-high grass in the pretty glade, stirring up small grasshoppers that jumped and whirred away out of our path. An African black kite wheeled and swooped overhead, possibly in the hope that we would scare out something for it to eat, such as a mouse or lizard. (Although how it would see small prey in the dense grass was beyond me.) I concentrated on locating the new road where it would best provide tourists with views of wildlife and scenic landscape. Being young and fanciful, I also occasionally daydreamed: "*The seasoned explorer bravely leads his men through the African wilds...*"

But with four laborers trailing after me muttering "*Polepole, tembo*" and "*polepole, nyati,*" I also could not help having large and cantankerous animals on my mind. So far, the open grassy area had been noticeably devoid of them, but what if one suddenly appeared and took exception to our presence? What would Bwana do then, eh? I also worried about snakes. The grass was so dense that I couldn't see what I was stepping on.

About midday we came to the end of the grassland. We were about to make our way into a large stand of crotalaria bushes at the edge of the bamboo when we heard a sudden, sharp *crack!* One of the bushes gave a great shake. (We stopped entering the crotalaria bushes.) Then we heard the rumble of an elephant's stomach. (We stopped even thinking about entering the crotalaria bushes.) Only then did it occur to me how long it had been since we'd left the D-4 driver to his own devices and how he probably needed our help. "*Twende kurudi*" I said. We are going back. They didn't argue. "*Ndiyo*" two of them agreed. Yes. A third said "*Twende upesi!*" Let's go quickly! The fourth didn't even bother to speak but promptly turned around and set off. An hour later, we discovered that the D-4 had broken down soon after we left it and hadn't worked since.

We spent two weeks putting in the new track. Three times, while engaged in sticking tall lengths of bamboo into the ground to mark where the new track would go, we jumped buffalo herds of forty to fifty animals. Luckily however, we scared them more than they scared us. What a noise they made as they blundered away grunting and snorting, heavy hooves rumbling across the ground—they were *big* animals. They always paused at the edge of the bamboo to look back at us. We could see the sun glinting off their horns. They were mean-looking critters!

From time to time we heard the snap of a breaking branch, or the sharp, thrilling sound of an elephant trumpeting inside the forest, so we knew that elephants were around. Then we saw some. We were in a glade, near where it edged up against the bamboo, when one of the men exclaimed, *"Tembo!"* A large elephant had unexpectedly materialized from the bamboo a few hundred feet away. Like a spirit, it moved silently across an arm of the glade and vaporized into the thicket on the other side. If the laborer hadn't happened to look up when he did, we would have missed it completely.

Almost immediately afterward, possibly because my senses had been sharpened by having just seen one, I noticed another elephant, or rather its tail, protruding from the bamboo. It was an odd-looking tail, too. Unlike most elephant tails, it was hairless. I was lucky to have seen it because we would otherwise have passed much too close for either the elephant's comfort or ours. We quickly backed up. Then we waited. As the air was moving in his direction it wasn't long before the beast realized that it had company. Quickly backing his way out of the bamboo, the elephant swung around and stood broadside to us for a few minutes, its trunk elevated to test the air. Fascinated in spite of myself—I was getting that *feeling* in my stomach—I stood and watched. Then, having sensed where we were, the elephant walked with a purposeful, loose-limbed stride across the field at a sharp angle away from us and tanked into the bamboo on the other side. Except for the lingering smell of elephant, and five people with big eyes and pulses returning to normal, the glade was empty again. I decided that further work in the bush would include someone with a gun.

Henry drove out to inspect our new track when it was finished. He liked it. Of course it was his idea to build it in the first place, but he liked the track's location, no doubt partly because he saw two eland, a reedbuck, a large herd of waterbuck, and two herds of buffaloes during the first drive along it. We were elated with *our* new track, which Henry named the Buffalo Ridge Track. It let tourists see big game animals in grassy glades, forest, and bamboo in one convenient circuit. We congratulated ourselves and sat back, figuratively speaking, to await compliments from happy users.

There weren't any. The track was seldom used. Henry and I were introduced to a basic law governing the suitability of a natural area for tourism in the Ngorongoro Conservation Area: tourists, most of whom spent only a single day in the area, preferred to spend that precious time in Ngorongoro Crater experiencing its wealth of wildlife in open savanna where visibility is in miles rather than feet. Not only that: Dhillon Singh complained that the large herd of buffalo which used to wallow every day in the mud next to the Forest Resort had not been seen since the track was built. Apparently occasional vehicles made them nervous. So we did not maintain the Buffalo Ridge Track, and in time it disappeared back into the original landscape.

The Wildlife Biologist

John Goddard lived next door to me with his petite wife Shelly, their cute four-year-old daughter Penny, and a small, shorthaired dog called Trixie. I spent a great deal of time with them, first because my gasoline ration was so restrictive I had lots of time to while away; and second, I liked them. John was a role model of sorts and Shelly, though younger than I, gave me motherly advice about girls. She probably thought I needed it because I was in my late twenties and still single.

Thirty-some years old, John was engaged in one of the first-ever studies of the black rhino. Funded by the Canadian Government, he could buy all the gas he needed, so when, for want of fuel, I couldn't do my own work, I often accompanied him into the field. Penny was too young for school, so the whole family often came too, even Trixie the dog, although regulations strictly forbade it. Not every family gets to bump cross-country with Dad in a four-wheel-drive Land Rover, get hissed to silence as he photographs a rhino before it charges, or eat lunch while a pride of lions dozes in the shade of their car. It seemed a good life. I envied them.

John kept track of his rhinos with a rogue's gallery of photographs. Each rhino was identifiable in the field by some unique set of characteristics such as frayed ears, scars, or the shape of the horn. He gave the rhinos names based on their looks and personalities and, in time, began to identify closely with them. They became part of his extended family. Shelly knew John's rhinos almost as well as her husband did, and their animated discussions about them could have been mistaken for gossip about their neighbors back home in Canada. More gregarious than her husband, Shelly enjoyed educating visitors about rhino behavior, providing nuggets of information with knowing, half-closed eyes, and slow nods of the head. For his part, I think John would have been happy if tourists and Maasai alike had been banned from the Conservation Area.

John was almost totally absorbed in his work. I rarely heard him talk about anything but rhinos. For instance: "Dennis, I'm worried about Gertrude; she's never been a mother before, and doesn't pay enough attention to her new calf." Or, "Homer's back again, with Betty over by the river; I'm surprised she hasn't chased him away." I remember once pouring out my soul to him on some fervently felt subject. He was quiet and looked interested. I *thought* he was listening. Then just before I reached my concluding and most telling point he interrupted: "Dennis, did you know that old George changed his territory today? It's the first time he's done that in two years!" John hadn't heard a word I'd said.

Henry, worried about a recent spate of rhino killings, had arranged for John's study. Although this was long ago, when poachers used spears rather than automatic weapons, there was yet reason for worry. The crater's rhino population seemed to be decreasing, and the conservation world was loudly complaining: newspaper and magazine editorials called for removal of the Maasai from the crater. Henry, however, felt that he needed a wildlife biologist to look into the matter first. His problem was that he couldn't afford one. But he got John Goddard, and this is how.

A year or so before my arrival, elements of the Tanganyika army mutinied against their British officers. At the request of the new government, British forces quickly quelled the insurrection. But in the meantime, mutinous soldiers spread fear and consternation around the town of Dodoma, in the center of the country. The Goddards, new arrivals in Dodoma where John was to work for the Tanganyika Department of Game, were forced from their house by angry soldiers, shouted at in an unintelligible language, and paraded about at bayonet point before being imprisoned. This decided them to leave Dodoma even if it meant returning to Canada. Thus it was that Henry received a telephone call from the Head of the Game Department who asked if he had any use for a fully funded wildlife biologist. John and his family arrived at Ngorongoro the following week.

Once Henry had explained his concerns about the rhino population, John set right to work photographing each new rhino that he encountered and marking their daily locations on a map. Over time, he could estimate the number of rhinos using the crater and the extent of each animal's home range. Births were recorded (and celebrated); deaths were recorded (and mourned). Collecting the skulls of dead rhinos, he examined the teeth to determine age at death. (The heads of dead animals were tossed into a forty-four gallon drum behind his house where they were cleaned by maggots. Viewing this process in full swing required a strong stomach.) He studied rhino behavior: How social were they? What happened when one encountered another? What were the mating rituals? Through this slow, methodical, detailed collecting of facts, John developed a picture of the relative health and vitality of the rhino population in the crater.

John discovered that there were more rhinos around than people thought. Most rhinos divided their time between the crater floor and the forest outside the crater. They came and went, and when they went, conservationists concluded they had been poached. Although the crater contained about ten rhino on any one day, John eventually found over a hundred that used it intermittently. This good news brought a collective sigh of relief from the Conservation Unit and the conservation world in general. Probably also from the Maasai living in the crater because they knew they were being blamed for the scarcity of rhinos, although I don't think their opinion on the matter was ever solicited.

Poaching did occur, but mostly in the forest. It was only noticed when a wounded rhino survived and returned to the crater floor, sometimes with the poacher's spear still in its side. These were the only times I ever saw John Goddard angry. He would storm into the office to pound on the conservator's desk, call down curses on the Maasai, and demand disciplinary action. John was particularly upset the day he discovered a baby rhino had been speared. Following that visit to the office, he was avoided for the next week by everyone from the conservator on down.

John watched what his rhinos ate (the professional term is *ingested*) in order to learn their food habits. Using binoculars, he watched what types of plants an animal delicately selected. After the rhino left, John searched the area for plants showing marks of browsing. At first John brought me the samples to identify. I was a forester; foresters deal with trees; trees are plants. Therefore I would know the names of all the grasses, herbs, and shrubs in Ngorongoro Crater.

After John discovered how few African plants I could name, he took his samples to the plant taxonomists at the East African Herbarium in Nairobi for identification. Here he encountered a different problem. Upon being presented with masticated, debarked, and withered plant remains, the taxonomist's all-too frequent response was to squeamishly hold the mess at arm's distance and say repressively: "These specimens are sterile!" (i.e., without fruits and/or flowers, the major structures taxonomists use for plant identification). It was made clear that just as one does not pick one's nose in church, neither does one present sterile plant materials to a plant taxonomist. However, both sides eventually made adjustments and John gradually accumulated a large number of named plant specimens. Attaching them to the leaves of a loose-leaf notebook with Scotch tape (which would have made a taxonomist wince), he carried them in the field as a botanical reference library.

John Goddard and game scout Tsitote outside the Ngorongoro Conservation Unit's offices with tusks recovered from a dead elephant. The bamboo-clad summit of Oldeani Mountain is in the background.

John also studied rhinos on the eastern Serengeti Plains. His family sometimes accompanied him. On a visit to his camp, a tent beneath a solitary umbrella acacia tree with an eye-catching view of the brown slopes and cedar-filled canyons of Makarut Mountain, I learned something about packing a Land Rover when taking one's family on safari. When it came time to return to Ngorongoro, the back end of the pickup was so full of gear (empty forty-four gallon water drums and gasoline jerry cans, large canvas tent, camp cots, mattresses, sleeping bags, camp table, safari chairs, dirty clothes, chop box, stove, and cooking utensils) that we had trouble squeezing in several rhino skulls that John had collected. I had John's camera box on my lap, a lantern between my feet, and Trixie the dog in front of the lantern;

Shelly had Penny and another lantern on her lap. Only John, who was driving, was relatively unencumbered, although he had to negotiate Shelly's knees when shifting gears. But no one seemed to mind. The Goddards liked camping together.

The Gorgor Swamp Track

Henry wanted to build another road, this time to open up an eight-mile strip between the southern crater wall and Gorgor Swamp. It would be a combined game-viewing track and firebreak to keep fires on the crater floor from sweeping up the wall into the forest.

This time I decided to ride with Paulu, the tractor driver, under the pretext that it would be easier this way to show him where to put the track. But what I really wanted was to experience the thrill of pushing dirt and rocks about—I half-envied Paulu because he did this every day. Climbing up beside him, I yelled over the engine's noise, "Let'er rip!" Then, seeing his blank stare, I tried again in Swahili: *"Twende."* Let's go, and off we clanked. Fifteen minutes later—fifteen minutes of thick, billowing dust, constant noise, and the machine's shaking, vibrating, thumping, and lurching—I viewed Paulu with more respect. The poor guy had to do this every day.

But the view was fine and I saw lots of zebra standing in wondering groups watching the roaring, clanking bulldozer go by. Only when I hopped down and showed myself separate from the machine did they take fright and drum away, barking and huffing. Vehicles were a curiosity; but humans were dangerous.

As were lions: "*Punda milia wanaona kitu!*" Paulu yelled at me over the sound of the engine. The zebras—literally, striped donkeys—see something!

Several very alert zebras were intently watching two female lions lying behind a patch of tall grass. Then I noticed that although the zebras were keeping a safe distance from the predators, we were not. We were heading right for the tawny, sharp-clawed beasts. Paulu, apparently feeling the situation needed clarifying, leaned over and yelled in my ear, "*Simba!*" Lion. So there I sat, with nothing between me and two lions but a lot of noise. I mean that tractor didn't even have a roof to protect its driver from falling tree branches; I thought up some choice things to say to Sambegi, the game scout, who hadn't shown up with his rifle for work this morning. But I needn't have worried, because just before we reached them, the lions turned and leisurely disappeared into the bush, apparently headed for the forest high on the crater wall. As I no longer wanted to ride the bulldozer and was under the impression that the area was now free of lions, I hopped down and went ahead for some distance, often out of sight of the bulldozer, not thinking about lions at all. Next morning, the discovery of a partially devoured zebra carcass on our newly cut track revealed this to have been the bliss of ignorance: lions had been present all the time. I had probably walked within a few feet of them without knowing it.

The bulldozer uncovered a snake one day; quite a pretty thing, really—light green, shading to white on the belly—and very streamlined. Fascinated, we watched as the slender reptile, tongue flickering, raised itself from the burrow, trying to make out what had disturbed its slumber. "*Nyoka! Mbaya sana!*" Sambegi shouted. Snake! Very bad! In a torrent of excited Swahili, he made me understand that if the snake, which he said was a green mamba (it wasn't, even I knew that) bit me I would not "*fika nyumbani*" or reach home. On its next pass, the tractor shoveled the snake out and we never saw it again.

The next day it was my turn to get excited. The game scout and I were some distance ahead of the tractor. I was leading by about fifty feet when I topped a small rise, spotted a large black object not far away, and danced nimbly back away again. *"Kifaru!"* Rhino! I hissed to Sambegi, who, warned by my precipitous retreat, had already jacked a round of ammunition into the breech of his rifle. Cautiously, he advanced up the rise with his rifle at the ready. Slowly, he looked over the other side. Then, he stood at the top of the rise and looked all around. Finally, all tension left his body and, grinning broadly, he turned to me. *"Mawe tu,"* he said. It's only a rock. Then, noticing the expression on my face, he kindly added, "But it's a big one."

Indignity struck again an hour later. We were seeing animals now: eland and kongoni at the edge of the swamp; five elephants high on the crater wall; a herd of eland and two waterbucks watching us closely from a quarter mile away. Then we almost ran into a cat or, more correctly, it almost ran into us. Twice the size of a house cat, it had a spotted coat, large ears, and long legs. *"Mondo,"* whispered Sambegi. It was a serval cat. Oblivious to our presence, the attractive little feline moved through the grass in our direction. Only when it was about fifty feet away did it briefly pause, taking us in with startled gaze, before bounding silently away.

Rather a small serval than a big leopard, I mused, although the game scout did have a rifle—Second World War issue, or maybe even older because it was bolt-action rather than semiautomatic. Briefly, I wondered what kind of service it had seen. Somme Offensive perhaps? Or maybe in the—

Sambegi shouted something that sounded like *"Nyuki!"* and threw himself to the ground. *"Nyuki?"* Yet another word I didn't know. Then I heard the humming. Suddenly, a cloud of bees—a swift-moving bundle of energy with high pain-inflicting potential—swept into view. I landed on my face next to the game scout, getting dust up my nose and grass in my hair. Maybe the bees wouldn't notice us as they buzzed by overhead. Sambegi and I stayed flat on the ground until the hum faded away and it was safe to stand again. Then we got up, brushed ourselves off—a box of matches in my shirt pocket had been flattened and my pipe had fallen into the grass—and congratulated ourselves on our escape: African bees are more aggressive than North American bees. And one bee can give repeated stings. I mentally added *nyuki* to my Swahili vocabulary.

We slept at Lerai Cabin, a small stone hut roofed with *mabati*, near the base of the crater wall overlooking Lerai Forest. Constructed before the First World War by a German farmer named Siedentopf, it was shaded by several large eucalyptus trees planted (probably) when the cabin was built. A friendly little stream murmured nearby, providing company.

It was a delightful setting, but we seldom had time to enjoy it because work usually started soon after sunrise and stopped just before sunset. The men took some cups of tea for breakfast. Then they didn't eat again—if a cup of tea is really eating—until they had their evening meal of *ugali* (oo-gall'-ee). They made *ugali* by pouring white maize flour into a *sufuria* of boiling water, vigorously stirring it with a long-handled wooden spoon until it was stiff. The cook of the day then upturned the *ugali* onto a large, brightly colored tin plate and placed it before the diners who pinched off a handful at a time (always with the right hand), balled it up, and popped it into the mouth. Sometimes they dipped it first into a small side dish of meat or vegetable stew (usually cabbage and tomatoes); but mostly, the men ate their *ugali* straight. It was too bland a diet for me even with the side dishes (imagine subsisting on stiff, unseasoned, mashed potatoes), but *ugali* was the principal food of most of the Africans in the country (although the Maasai traditionally subsisted on milk, sometimes mixed with cow's blood).

About a week into the job, I received a visit from John Goddard and his family who came to see how the track was progressing. Naturally John used the occasion to get a little of his own work done. Together, he and I climbed into a sturdy acacia and searched the terrain for rhino.

We saw three right away, one a young calf. Also in sight were sixteen elephants shouldering their way through the shrubs down to the swamp. But John focused his camera entirely on the rhinos. Not having seen these individuals before, he was ecstatic.

"Amazing! [*Click.*] Look at the horns on that one. [*Click.*] That *mtoto*—baby—must be about three months old. [*Click, click ... click.*] Wonder why I've never seen them before. Are these the ones you saw this morning? [*Click.*] Look at the scar on the female's side. Unbelievable! [*Click.*] She's been fighting for sure, Dennis. [*Click ... click.*] Fantastic!" [*Click.*]

As usual, John was happily caught up in his work. And I was happy that he was happy. However, it was late afternoon, and I had seen quite enough wildlife for the day, including a large bull elephant with tusks so long they almost touched the ground. I left John to commune with his rhinos and climbed down to walk through the lippia bushes to where his wife and daughter were waiting in the car. I needed a drink of water and some conversation about something besides rhinos.

"Dennis!" John yelled from high in the tree. "Run for the car!"

I had been walking towards the car anyway, where Shelly and Penny were waiting; but now I whirled in alarm. About a hundred yards away, John was in trouble.

"Leopard!" He shouted while frantically breaking off a dead branch to use as a club. "At the base of the tree!"

John had been treed by a leopard once before, in Lerai Forest. He had also fallen from a tree into some needle-tipped sansevieria plants at Oldupai Gorge, been charged by an elephant while on foot searching for rhino skulls near Ngorongoro settlement, and was once chased about by ostriches defending their nest in the crater. He led an interesting life, and I rather admired him for it. I just wished he wouldn't involve me in its more-exciting parts.

He had this time, however. There he was, as high in the tree as he could get, shouting excitedly and waving his improvised club; the leopard was probably this very moment preparing to bound up the tree and chew his ankles off. Impulsively, I picked up a rock and ran toward the tree; maybe some loud screams and a rock bounced off its noggin would scare the beast away (I could do a good scream). Halfway there my mind finally started functioning. Running back to John's Land Rover, which luckily still had the keys in its ignition, I drove it through the bushes towards the tree while Shelly tried to calm Penny's anxious queries about her father's safety. But we never saw the leopard. The noise of our approach—racing engine, the screech and whap of branches against the car, wheels thumping over rough terrain—probably scared it off. John clambered down as fast as he could and we returned to the road. By this time Shelly had had enough. She had not slept well at Munge Camp. She had almost stepped on a cobra earlier in the morning. And now the leopard. It was time to go home.

And home they went.

Three days later I staked the point where the new track was to join the main tourist road about half a mile north of Koitoktok Forest. I stood listening to the muted growl of the tractor in the distance while watching a secretary bird stalk through the grass looking for lizards and snakes. Overhead, a column of vultures silently wheeled and soared, taking advantage of a mid-afternoon thermal. Although not as exciting as the Goddards' visit, the last few days had had their moments, especially yesterday, when a herd of twenty-eight elephants, spooked by our presence, rapidly retreated up a low ridge, stopping to test the air with trunks held high like snorkels before trumpeting shrilly and shoving off again. Two tiny youngsters scuttled along behind, doing their best to keep up. Then, in Koitoktok Forest, where zebra grazed beneath large, widely spaced fever trees, we discovered a brush-walled enclosure with five small grass huts. Sambegi, the game scout, explained that this was a Maasai ritual site where the warriors came to eat meat. "Women are forbidden!" he added with a meaningful look.

While waiting for John, who had promised to return today and pick me up, I daydreamed about hot water, clean clothes, and decent food. Eventually his Land Rover emerged from Koitoktok Forest following the line of marker stakes I had left: clearly, John was already using the new track to look for rhinos. I hopped aboard gratefully. Home was less than an hour away and Daniel, my cook and houseboy, knew I was coming, so I would soon be enjoying a hot bath.

I should have known better.

Less than a mile down the road John stopped the car, whipped out his binoculars, and trained them on something at the edge of Gorgor Swamp.

"Rhino," he pronounced. "This might be a new one, Dennis. You do the driving. I want my hands free to take photos."

Grudgingly, I switched with him and drove toward the black dot that was a rhino. The grass became greener, taller and denser until it resembled a rug with bumper-high pile. It obscured depressions and holes that I wanted to avoid, so I slowed down. Then, as we neared the rhino, I drove even slower so we wouldn't frighten it away.

"It's Gertrude!" John exclaimed as he dropped his binoculars and grabbed his camera. "And she has a calf! Fantastic!" Hurriedly, he attached a telephoto lens and instructed me to drive closer.

"Way out of her normal range. [*Click*.] More to the right, Dennis, keep going. *Yes!* [*Click*.] Maybe she came to give birth in the cover of the reeds. [*Click, click*.] This makes three baby rhinos this year. Amazing. [*Click*.] Damn! Stop a minute while I reload. Oh stay there baby, please, I need some more shots—why can't they make these things easier to load! [*Snap, click, click, click*.] Okay, closer now. I need a good head shot of the little guy for my files."

The next moment was a blur during which the only thing we both saw clearly was that there would be no close-up shot of the new baby's head. Mom was charging.

"Get us out of here, Dennis! Fast!"

As if I needed instructions along those lines. It was like the classic bad dream where the monster is chasing you and you just can't move. I wrenched desperately at the steering wheel and pushed the gas pedal to the floor but the rhino kept getting closer and larger. *Whump!* The Land Rover hit a hyena hole and bounced; briefly, both of us left our seats. John's foam rubber-lined camera equipment case, which he had placed on the seat between us, fell to the floor. Camera lenses and film containers rolled about at our feet. But John didn't notice.

"Faster!"

"Here she comes!"

"Watch out!"

Then she hit us. *Bump*! Bump? I thought as I finally got the Land Rover pointed in the right direction and up to speed. *Wham!* The vehicle hit another hole concealed in the grass. We really went airborne this time: all four wheels left the ground; the Land Rover's hood came unlatched; and John's photographic equipment rearranged itself, the camera case catching upside down on the four-wheel-drive gearshift. But Mama wasn't after us any more.

When we were far enough away to safely stop, we found a small dent in the left rear body of the car. I was vaguely disappointed. Of course I was pleased that no serious damage had occurred. But, still. *Bump?*

We returned to Ngorongoro without further mishaps and I quickly headed for the bathtub. Later, while soaking in the hot water, I concluded that going on safari with John Goddard was a sure cure for boredom. I wondered idly when the next treatment would be.

How Not to View an Elephant

I tripped and slammed against John Goddard's parked Land Rover pickup. Quickly recovering from my stumble, I bruised a shin scrambling into the cab, but didn't realize it until later. Banging the door shut I found John had somehow overtaken me in the race to the pickup and was already in the driver's seat, wrenching at the ignition switch and yanking the gearshift into place. The pickup bounced and lurched as the rest of the group piled into the open back. The next big bounce would come when four or five tons of elephant hit us with murderous intent. *It was time to go!*

But, we didn't. The elephant never came. Just as John released the clutch to get the heck out of there, I looked back expecting to see a window full of disgruntled elephant and found—nothing. The animal was still back in the meadow, phlegmatically poking about in the grass with its trunk and pulling up occasional large clumps to eat. It looked smug.

John and I were returning to Ngorongoro from Arusha, accompanied by some junior staff and their relatives riding in the back of John's pickup. Driving up through the forest reserve, we attained the crater rim and headed toward Ngorongoro. That was when we saw the elephant.

The animal was the sole occupant of a meadow. Turning off the engine, John picked up his ever-present binoculars and spent some time watching the elephant, which, he said, had some interesting ear and tusk features. Then he surprised me. Instead of entering his observations in his little notebook and continuing down the road, he sat ruminating for a few minutes and then said, "Let's walk over and get a closer look!"

Now, I wanted to do that about as much as I wanted to pet a leopard with a toothache. However, not wanting to appear a wimp, I said, "Why, sure. Let's do that." I got out and followed John towards the elephant, trying to look as confident as he appeared to be.

We crossed a shallow, muddy depression and strode across the grassy field to where the large animal, which was, I suppose, a hundred feet away, seemed very decidedly to "loom." Only then did we stop and I discover that our passengers, two men, and a woman nursing a small child, had followed us. They must have reasoned that if the two white bwanas weren't afraid then neither should they be. It was touching, such confidence, but in my opinion, pretty naïve.

John revealed the reason for our excursion when he knelt to investigate some clumps of herbaceous vegetation. "Look, Dennis, it was eating star grass—and a clover. Didn't know they even grew here; all I ever see from the road is manyatta grass." Rising to his feet, he focused once more on the elephant. "Wish he'd move," he said. "Then we could check over there, too." If John was a typical wildlife biologist, I suspected they mostly died young.

The elephant just stood there gently swaying, ears idly flapping, pulling up an occasional tussock of grass to eat (banging it first against its leg to remove the dirt from the roots). It gave no indication that our presence bothered it. Still, I worried. Surely, despite its tonnage, it could catch us if it wanted to.

Then, perhaps because we were so close to one, John decided to lecture us about elephants. Did you know that its ears are part of the elephant's cooling system? That's why elephants flap their ears so much. Did you know that elephants have inefficient digestive systems? That's why they must eat frequently and in large amounts. Did you know that some elephants don't have tusks?

I hadn't known, and in another setting might have been interested. Just now, however, I couldn't stop thinking about those tusks, tusks that were chipped and smoothed from digging, ripping, and gouging things. Then I remembered a story about a white hunter who, after his rifle misfired, was pinned between an elephant's tusks when the enraged animal tried to squish him against the ground. He survived only because the tusks were so long they couldn't penetrate all the way into the soil. (Suddenly, the tusks of our elephant seemed to shorten.)

The Africans in our group, however, were interested. One of the men alternated between translating for the others and asking about the weight, quality, and market price of the tusks, which made me wonder if he might be planning to do some poaching. The other fellow, who looked like someone's great-grandfather, made polite listening noises and told us about elephants raiding his maize fields over the years. But it was the woman who made the greatest impression. Holding her baby up so that it could see the elephant, she cried in Swahili, "Child, look! This is the elephant that killed your father!" Then she calmly resumed suckling the infant while the rest of us stared at her in fascinated horror.

John, taking her literally, hastened to correct her misconception. Learning from the translator that her husband had died far away in another part of the country, he told her that this elephant could not be his killer. Furthermore, elephants were dangerous only if they felt threatened. Hunting was forbidden in the Ngorongoro Conservation Area, and elephants were not harassed. Therefore she was not to upset herself (she didn't look upset), we were safe. At this point, the elephant suddenly turned on us and charged.

Now here we were, back in the Land Rover after our swift passage across the meadow, pulses racing, puffing like marathon runners, while the car continued to gently bounce and sway from the impact of its occupants' sudden arrival. However, we were safe; the elephant had not followed through with its charge. It was time for us to go home, reflect on our providential escape, and begin fine-tuning our story which, I thought, had some potential. I looked at John. He had this funny look in his eye and it was not a look associated with going home and having tea. My heart sank. And sure enough, John got out and walked back towards the elephant, followed I might add, by everyone from the back of the pickup.

I eventually got out and followed along behind, but I grumped to myself the whole way. I was so deeply immersed in my sulk as I crossed the muddy depression and trudged through the grass that I paid little attention to what was going on up ahead. Therefore, I was completely caught off guard by the sudden cries of dismay to my front; the blurred passage, at great speed, of several people returning to the truck, and the discovery that I had suddenly become the closest person to the elephant, which was in full charge.

Well, I didn't reach the car first this time, either, but I gave it a very good try. Despite disparities in age, gender, and footwear (the Africans were wearing flip-flops), and the fact that the others had a head start on me, we reached the car in a tight little group. People piled pell-mell into the back—the child was tossed aboard—as I yanked open the car door and bundled into the front and John started the car, stomped on the accelerator, and spun out down the road. The last man to dive aboard still had his legs hanging over the tailgate. I looked back as we sped away. The elephant, having successfully "seen us off the premises," had pulled up just short of the muddy depression (where a single flip-flop sandal stood upright, abandoned in the mud). The big animal had only wanted a bit of peace.

This time we went home.

The Game Scouts and Their Boss

Close encounters with dangerous wildlife were exciting but this didn't make me want to repeat them. To minimize my chances of being mauled, stomped, or gored, I had an armed game scout accompany me on foot safaris.

The Ngorongoro Conservation Unit employed a number of game scouts to enforce the game laws and control (i.e., shoot) particularly troublesome animals, such as crop-destroying elephants or cattle-killing lions. The scouts were a mix of local Maasai and Wambulu, and incomers from elsewhere in the country. Stationed in one's and two's at small guard posts throughout the Conservation Area, they patrolled on foot. Transport difficulties, including frequent fuel shortages, limited supervision by the assistant conservator (game). This probably encouraged them to skip anti-poaching patrols, but it also meant that whenever I appeared at a guard station needing a game scout, there was usually one there. They served me well, too.

As, for instance, the time in the Laianai Forest, north of the crater, when my game scout escort, who was walking ahead of me, stopped to listen to something. Then, motioning me to silence, he moved deeper into the thicket where he slowly parted the branches of a shrub and, with a nod, indicated that I should look. I saw gray—elephant gray. The animal was so close that I could see flies moving about on its skin. Enveloped in pachyderm smell we stood for a minute, watching patterns of shade and light shift about on its wrinkled skin before carefully letting the branches slip back in place. Then we stole away, leaving the elephant to its dreams.

Another time, a game scout and I were in a part of the Lerai Forest where the tall fever trees were in various stages of senility. We climbed into the ten-to twelve-feet-high, now almost-horizontal branches of a downed tree to get a view of the surrounding area. Seeing nothing, we were about to climb down again when the scout nudged me and pointed to a rhino that had just emerged from the shrubbery. Alert to our presence, the rhino held its head up as it tried to hear or smell us (rhinos have poor eyesight). Then, raising a flurry of oxpecker birds that had been resting on its back, it quickly swiveled to repeat the pose in another direction. Eventually, the rhino, unable to find us, began to feed. Some minutes later it disappeared into a stand of stiff, head-high, orange-flowered leonotis and we got down and returned to our Land Rover parked at the edge of the forest.

Now that's the way to see wildlife!

I felt no apprehension during these excursions. Not knowing any better, I assumed the game scouts to be experienced woodsmen with sharp senses. They had been shooting big game animals for years as part of their game control duties (or so I understood), so they also would be expert marksmen. I knew my escorts would either keep me away from dangerous animals in the first place, or, if worse came to worst, they would just shoot them. I was content.

That is, until I watched the game scouts at their annual target practice. They placed several targets against a hill and, under the supervision of the chief game scout, blazed away at them for over an hour with their war surplus 303's. I'd never seen such awful shooting! Just to check, I fired several of the rifles myself and had no problem hitting the targets—I was the best shot there! From then on I relied on the scouts' alertness and keen eyes to keep me out of trouble. For whatever good it might do, I often carried the rifle myself.

It worked. Despite being duds at shooting, the game scouts were experts at keeping me out of trouble. I was able to continue my excursions with a comparatively peaceful state of mind—often with a rifle slung over my shoulder.

In 1966, the Tanganyika Game Department seconded yet another game warden to the Ngorongoro Conservation Unit to be its new assistant conservator (game). The post had a high turnover rate, which probably reflected the government's unsettled administrative situation. The departure of many experienced British officials was causing a flurry of personnel adjustments in all agencies, including frequent shifts of people from place to place. In the case of Ngorongoro, the average stay of game wardens was only a few months.

Most game wardens were British citizens, locally born or in-comers to East Africa after the Second World War. Many had been professional hunters who took well-heeled Americans and Europeans on big game hunting safaris. Some were white settlers. All had served during the Second World War, and, after that a few had been with the Kenya Regiment during the Mau Mau insurrection. Game wardens tended to be tough, rugged individuals. Some were real characters.

We got one of those. "What the bloody hell is this?" roared the new AC(G), his voice booming through the knot holes and cracks in the wooden partition separating our respective offices; having just been ushered into his by the Head Game Scout, he was clearly unimpressed. Next door, Forester Sheka Busalu and I perked up and paid attention. Our report on the continued high losses of plantation eucalyptus trees to girdling by buffalo could wait; this was more interesting. "How can I work in this confounded mess?" the voice continued irritably. "Absolute rot! What's that? Speak up, damn it!—*No*!" And thus it went for twenty minutes or so, accompanied by the thumps, bumps, and scrapes of moving furniture as the new man took the measure of his new and apparently unsatisfactory surroundings. Then with a barked, "Damn conservator shall hear about this," he exited the office with a slam of the door, to clump away across the compound still muttering to himself about the various inadequacies of his new situation. I gave him four months.

His name was Oscar Charleton, and he proved me wrong by lasting a full twelve months before a medical disability forced him into retirement. Fortunately, what Mr. Busalu and I heard that morning was only one, infrequently experienced facet of Oscar's personality. Occasionally highly strung and nervous, he proved, for the most part, to be a pleasant gentleman with Old World manners, especially around children and ladies. A colleague's wife still fondly remembers Oscar's effusive compliments after dining with them one night.

A slender, slightly hunched, middle-aged bachelor of medium height and sandy hair, Oscar affected a pointed, handle bar moustache with an upward twist at the end. He wore a tweed jacket and khaki shorts which were just barely visible beneath the jacket. His legs were long and skinny, and he wore calf-length brown knit cotton stockings into the top of which he clipped two ballpoint pens. Probably wore a tie too—I no longer remember but I bet he did. Recognizably English, Oscar so resembled an aged version of a World War II RAF officer that I was unsurprised to learn, years later (Oscar never spoke to me about his wartime experiences), that he actually had been one. A navigator in the Pathfinders, a special unit that flew ahead of the main group of bombers to mark the target, he flew numerous missions over Germany before being shot down and interned. As a POW he was roughly treated, which may explain why he was sometimes nervy.

After the war Oscar worked in central and southern Africa before moving to Tanganyika. He had been both a game ranger (the old title for game warden) involved in anti-poaching activities, and a game control officer who protected crops, property, and lives from the ravages of wildlife. With fourteen years' experience under his belt, he was an old African hand.

Unlike the other assistant conservators, Oscar owned his own private vehicle, a small short-wheel-base Land Rover, which I greatly coveted. Noticing me enviously inspecting it one day—I was without official transport again—he emerged from his house and sidled up beside me.

"Proper *gari* eh?" he said, giving his moustache a complacent twist. "Had it fitted out for my rifle, full safari kit, and cook, you know; just the thing for getting out of the office." (I'd suspected he wasn't an office person.) With a grin he nudged me in the ribs. "And believe me, old chap, nobody can find me when I go, either, know what I mean?"

I knew; I envied him for that, too.

Maybe because we were both bachelors, Oscar and I got along. He liked to talk. When I had time on my hands I would go over to his place, and he would tell me about his experiences in the bush, while cleaning his treasured double-barreled elephant gun. Some of the stories may even have been true, but I suspect Oscar probably was more interested in their effect on the listener than in their veracity. One of the more-amusing concerned his activities as a game control officer in Northern Rhodesia (Zambia).

It was the policy in central Africa to eliminate all wild game in blocks of land adjacent to agricultural and ranching areas in order to control the spread of trypanosomiasis (sleeping sickness). Many game species such as buffalo, wildebeest, and giraffe carry parasites called trypanosomes which, when transmitted by *tsetse* and other biting flies, cause sleeping sickness in humans, and the equally dreaded *nagana* disease in cattle. Killing all the game animals in an area eliminated *tsetse* flies and, therefore, trypanosomiasis, by removing their food supply. An effective method of tsetse control, it was greatly disliked by many people, including Oscar, who considered it unnecessarily brutal and wasteful.

As a game control officer, Oscar was forced to participate in this eradication program. His objections were, he said, loud and lengthy, but to no avail: it was a take it or leave it situation and he needed the work. His superiors allocated him a large block of land to clear of game animals, gave him funds to finance his work, and instructed him to get on with the job whether he liked it or not. One afternoon as we relaxed in his living room after work, he told me how he did it.

"Took care of 'em, I did," Oscar waved an already well-used bottle of gin at me. "Sure you won't have a snort Den? Spent a full year out there, trained up my own people of course, hired them from the local villages. Found an old *askari* the Germans had trained in Tanganyika during the First World War. Had him drill those scoundrels and he didn't know a word of English, just German. Excellent chap! Top notch! By year's end, they were the sharpest-looking bunch of German-speaking game scouts in all of Northern Rhodesia. Animals? Control? You know something Den? They never did learn to shoot, so I couldn't possibly send them out, could I? I hired that *askari* because he could drill, not shoot. And he couldn't shoot worth a damn! Hah, hah, hah! Come on Den, have a drink. Gin's good for you. No? Well, I'll have one myself then."

For a few minutes, Oscar pensively stared out the window, probably recalling the good old days. Then he grinned.

"Of course, the bastards didn't renew my contract—their loss, what? So, I came to Tanganyika … Den, I'm worried about you. Here, old boy, let me pour you [holding the bottle up to the light]—why, the damn thing's empty!"

As game warden his principal job had been to chase, catch, and prosecute poachers. He liked the prosecuting part best. One of his more-frequently-told stories was about the friendly magistrate, probably a fellow member of the local expatriates club, who called him aside after a successful prosecution and mentioned that the piece of giraffe skin used as evidence to convict the defendant seemed familiar from several previous prosecutions. Oscar should replace it with something else, he warned, as the public might eventually notice. Besides, it was beginning to smell. This story always ended with Oscar slapping his thighs and loudly guffawing. Then, giving his moustache another twist or two he would go on to the next story.

A gallant with the ladies whenever the opportunity arose, Oscar once invited me to accompany him and two attractive tourists into the crater. During the drive, Oscar played his role as the rugged, bush-wise game warden to the hilt.

Noticing several buffaloes in a draw on the crater rim, he casually observed, "Mmm yes, buffs. Cunning chaps, circle round in dense bush and get you from behind. Potted one once near Nachingwea. Took two direct hits from my .470. Died just in front of me. Looked around for my gun bearer. He'd fled of course. Can't trust these chaps in emergencies you know, eh, what?" Removing a hand from the steering wheel, he stoked his moustache.

The women, never having met a white hunter game warden before, were intrigued.

As we approached a pride of lions, Oscar declared, "Remarkably nice *simbas*, these. Shot a big black mane once, been killing native cows you know, around Singida. First shot bang through the heart, but it mauled three natives before it died. Splendid animal!" An elephant sighted at the edge of Lerai Forest brought forth a story about a big tusker Oscar had shot in Southern Rhodesia. A wart hog trotting away from the car reminded him of a necklace of wart hog tusks given him by a grateful chief for shooting a bothersome leopard. And, so it went. The women hung on every word.

Encouraged, Oscar suggested showing them the proper way

to shoot a rifle. He stopped the car, extracted from the back a .303 rifle borrowed that morning from the departmental storeroom at Ngorongoro, and lectured us on how to aim and fire it. Then, drawing our attention to a stick lying on the ground some distance away, he casually pulled down on it while the women covered their ears and waited for the stick to spin away in a puff of dust. However, instead of the expected loud *crack* of a bullet exploding out of the barrel, we heard a hollow *click*—*sproing* and the rifle's metal base plate fell out and hung, jiggling up and down, at the end of a long spring.

Since it's hard to impress anyone once they've seen the bottom of your rifle fall out, Oscar ended the tour there and then. Even young women from deepest London know that real he-man game wardens who routinely shoot rogue elephants, tie venomous snakes in knots with their bare hands, and bully villainous poachers, don't have rifles that go *click*—*sproing* and dangle their base plates; the rifles wouldn't dare. We went directly home. There were no drinks with impressionable young women at the lodge that night, either.

Oscar had not come to Ngorongoro by choice. His previous posting had been to Tanga, a sleepy little town on the north coast with a nice club where he could sit at the bar and drink and talk with like-minded British expatriates. He may have sensed that his posting to Ngorongoro was a prelude to replacement by an African. With no job experience beyond World War II soldiering, shooting game, and chasing poachers, he would find it hard to get work in Britain. Having to take orders from an African superior—Solomon ole Saibull was now conservator—may also have had something to do with it. Many old colonials found this difficult. Whatever the reason, Oscar didn't like it here. Nevertheless, he soldiered on.

An elephant at the edge of Lerai Forest shakes its head, creating a cloud of dust.

Game scout Sambegi on a sand dune in the Angata Salei or Salei Plain. The Crater Highlands rise in the distance.

Life on the Crater Rim

Buffaloes by My Bedroom

I lived in the Conservation Unit's old guest house, a small cement-block building with corrugated tin roof and dinky porch. The kitchen stood separate from the house, across a grassy yard that was grazed at night by buffaloes. They didn't just graze, either. One moonlit night about 2 a.m., I awoke to find two hefty bulls fighting outside my bedroom window. Grunting and panting, they pushed one another back and forth, digging up divots of grass and flattening bushes. One, shoved backward by the impact of its opponent's charge, thudded against the house. The other slipped and fell on its hindquarters but quickly recovered. Flanks heaving and drool dripping from their muzzles, they rested briefly before the larger of the pair gave a great bawl and charged again. The two bulls raged about the yard for some time in a struggle that would have made marvelous television. I just wanted them to go away and let me sleep.

The rooms of the house—a main room, two bedrooms, and a bathroom—didn't interconnect. Instead, each opened directly onto the yard. On foggy mornings, after carefully checking for the presence of buffaloes, I groped my way to the bathroom through heavy mist. At night, I checked again with a flashlight before going to bed.

Logs burning in the fireplace warmed the main room on cold days and kept it dry, an attribute that, one day, introduced me to an interesting bit of botanical natural history. While reading by the fire I was startled by a sharp *pop*. A small object the size of a shotgun pellet hit the book and rolled into my lap. Then—pop, pop, pop, pop, pop—more explosions; pellets filled the room, bouncing across the floor and ricocheting off the walls like shrapnel. Several weeks before, I had placed a fruiting segment of a branch of a tree euphorbia on a cupboard top and then forgotten it. The seeds had come to maturity in the warm, dry room. Now they were being dispersed, just as they would in the wild, not by dropping to the ground, or floating away in the wind, but by exploding out of their enclosing capsules.

Water was piped in from a spring on Oldeani Mountain. A wood-fired Tanganyika boiler—two forty-four gallon drums mounted one atop the other and connected by galvanized piping—heated it, providing boiling hot water that popped and hissed from a ten-foot-high overflow pipe (shaped like a shepherd's crook) at the most unexpected moments to spray unwary passersby. The piped water serviced a flush toilet and one of those really old bathtubs with iron legs cast in the form of eagle talons clutching a ball. The tub was so long and deep I could stretch out and submerge in it (and I'm not small). And I frequently did, too, except when the pipes in the forest broke or large animals dirtied the water by mucking about in the spring.

I sometimes became frustrated or even angry working at Ngorongoro, but seldom for long. My house, although small and lacking electricity, had much to do with it, as did its wonderful setting. Together they acted to overcome my petty moods. I remember one time in particular.

Solomon ole Saibull and I started it all off with a spirited disagreement about something. I left his office fuming. Picking up the mail, I found that two rolls of film containing fabulous scenes, unlikely to be encountered again (including a pack of wild dogs—Cape hunting dogs—bringing down a gazelle), had returned from the developer overexposed. Then I discovered to my dismay that most of the plant specimens I had collected over the last several months for the Conservation Unit's reference herbarium were useless. I hadn't changed the newspapers between the plants often enough and the plants never dried out. Plant after plant was either moldy or just disintegrated into little pieces when picked up. I felt like an old employee upon learning that his company's pension scheme no longer existed. All that time and effort wasted. *Wasted*!

Then, in quick succession, I failed a driver's test in Arusha, which I had fully expected to pass; missed my ride home; witnessed an unedifying tussle between the bus conductor and a passenger who couldn't pay his fare; and arrived at Ngorongoro to find a locked house and no one around, such as Daniel, my cook, or Philip, the other resident of the house, who might have the keys. Cold ashes in the maw of the Tanganyika boiler indicated there would be no hot water that night either. Bah!

Some time later, after tracking down an extra set of keys, I sat morosely by the fire—which I'd had to build *myself!*—eating something cold directly from the tin and feeling like Job (what would go wrong next, boils?). But then I tried to look on the good side: a cheerful fire was warming the room; my short-wave radio was playing something soothing from the BBC; and I would sleep in my own bed tonight. Tomorrow would be better.

But that was the night the two buffaloes chose to fight outside my bedroom window, so I awoke the next morning tired and grumpy. As I slowly eased out of bed and got the room into focus, I wondered if I shouldn't just go back to sleep and let the day continue without me. Then I saw the pile of newspaper sheets containing my ruined plant

My house.

specimens moldering away in the corner of the bedroom and my mood instantly worsened. Fed up with things going wrong, I decided to give Daniel a fearsome chewing-out for slacking off yesterday. Pulling on my clothes, I yanked open the bedroom door and stamped outside.

Grass, hedge, buildings, and trees glowed orange and yellow in the early moments of sunrise, the colors blending into a dreamlike, almost surreal scene. I stood transfixed as the unearthly colors gradually sharpened, contrasts and shadows appeared, and the dream scene changed into a normal, brightly lit sunrise. Then I noticed the fire crackling away under the bottom drum of the Tanganyika boiler and, joy of joys, steaming water spitting out of the overflow pipe—I could have a bath! Daniel was back on the job again. I immediately forgave him (actually, now that I thought about it, I might not have told him when to expect me back). Wasting no time, I filled the bathtub and had a luxurious, skin-wrinkling soak.

Afterward, I viewed my surroundings with a more-appreciative eye. The day was sunny, the morning air pleasantly cool, and dewdrops in the grass sparkled like jewels. Birds enlivened the scene with color and movement: a Tacazze sunbird, iridescent black, metallic violet, or bronze, depending on its angle to the sun, flitted about, poking its scimitar-shaped bill into brightly colored flowers; a Fiscal Shrike, looking like a black-hooded executioner, perched atop a fence post waiting for an unsuspecting insect to appear. Nearby, someone was chopping wood—*thunk ... thunk ... thunk*—but, otherwise, the morning was pleasantly quiet. Next door, the Goddard family was probably still in bed.

Then I noticed clouds on the eastern rim of the crater ten miles away. It was the monsoon season when clouds pile against the Crater Highlands, and whenever conditions are right they spill over the seven thousand-foot-high eastern rim into Ngorongoro Crater. Sometimes they flow smoothly like water spilling over a dam, while at other times they boil and foam like dry ice. This morning, cottony white clouds were drifting in fragile fingers down the inner slope of the crater to disappear magically into thin air, soaked up by the warmer, drier air near the crater floor.

For several minutes I stood immobilized by this meteorological vanishing act before a movement a few hundred feet away diverted my attention. It was a lone buffalo, probably one of last night's contestants, limping through the bushes. Magnanimously, I forgave it for interrupting my sleep last night, and turned my thoughts to breakfast. Maybe I would survive the day after all.

Daniel, my cook, lived in a two-room hut behind the kitchen. Daniel also was my house boy. Actually, he wasn't a boy at all but a grown man about twenty-five years old. "House boy" was a colonial term for African men hired to do domestic work (the women kept to agriculture and childbearing). The term had nothing to do with age; old grandfathers shuffling in with the afternoon tea tray were still "house boys."

Daniel, a member of the Warusha tribe, was one of an increasing number of Africans who no longer had land to till and had to look for work elsewhere. He found it with me. About my size, Daniel was a wiry, serious man. He was a quiet person, which is to say that he seldom played his radio at full volume or held conversations as though his audience was half a mile away. Neither did he have many friends and relatives hanging around getting in my way. He also knew how to wash and iron clothes and cook a few basic meals, so he fit my limited needs as a young bachelor very well.

He could smile—I remember his doing it once or twice—but he wasn't known for it. This might just have been his character, but it also reflected his marriage which, while it lasted, was unhappy. It was a "mixed" marriage, his wife, an Mbulu, being from a different tribe. A married couple from different tribes not only had to adapt to one another's personal idiosyncrasies, but also to unfamiliar cultural expectations and prejudices.

However, Daniel probably contributed to his marital difficulties. For instance, he didn't carry out all of his wedding commitments, to wit: two gifts of money to his bride's parents so that they could throw celebratory parties. According to the custom of her tribe, this put him in danger of losing both his wife and children. To help him out I bought part- interest in the marriage by shelling out seventy shillings, a lot of money in those days. But after one of their arguments escalated to physical violence, she decamped for good, leaving him with the children. I not only lost the seventy shillings but also had to convince Daniel that my contribution had been a one-time sort of thing and not a permanent raise in his salary.

Daniel and I got on well. Only a few times did he give me any trouble, such as the day the game scouts gave me a large piece of zebra meat confiscated from a poacher. They left it in my kitchen while I was at the office. When I came home, I found this big chunk of fresh red meat, black-and-white-striped skin still adhering to one side, staining the kitchen counter and dripping blood on the floor. I also found Daniel, who was so agitated that he forgot to speak English and rattled away instead in Swahili. Zebra meat would kill me if I ate it, and it would do so quickly. What did the person who left it think he was doing? Even to touch it was dangerous! No way was he going to cook it for me! Did I want him jailed as my murderer? (Apparently, the Warusha have this thing about zebra meat.) I ate no zebra meat that night. Instead, I heaved it over the fence into the bushes where, no doubt, some passing hyena made a quick meal of it. Hyenas don't have hang-ups about what they eat.

Visitors, of which I had many, had to sleep on the floor because Philip ole Sayalel, a conservation assistant, had the extra bedroom. Employed by the Ngorongoro Conservation Unit soon after my arrival, he had come to me looking for a place to stay. Philip combined the tall, slim body and narrow features of the classic Maasai with a shy, Jimmy Stewart-like grin. He was unusual in that he was an educated Maasai (roughly high school level plus a two-year diploma in animal husbandry). This was because his father, the government-appointed chief at Longido near the Kenya border, chose which children in his district had to attend school. You will notice the words "had to." Unlike many other tribes in the country, the Maasai did not approve of wasting their children by sending them to school. Nonetheless, a few had to go to satisfy a government-mandated quota of students from each Maasai district. The Maasai of Longido District, unhappy about sending any children at all, made certain the chief shared their misfortune by including one of his own. He chose Philip.

At first Philip hated school. But he eventually adjusted. Now, whenever he visited his parents' *boma*, to trade shirt and trousers for a traditional *shuka*, drink fresh warm milk direct from the cow, and watch his personal herd of cattle, given into the care of a relative, return lowing and bawling to the *boma* at night, he did so knowing that he could never return permanently to traditional life. The break had been too complete. I discovered how serious Philip was about this when I returned from safari one evening to find him lying in bed, weak from loss of blood. He had decided the large earring hole in his ear lobe did not fit with modern life and had stitched it up—all by himself, with no anesthetic.

When he could get transport, Philip spent his time in the field doing things like counting livestock. This made him unpopular with the Maasai, because they suspected (wrongly, in this case, as it was for ecological and veterinary reasons) that anyone interested in the size of their herds had to be a tax collector. Livestock was taxable property and, like everyone else in the world, the Maasai tried to minimize their taxes. No herder ever willingly divulged the true extent of his holdings, so Philip encountered considerable resistance, especially from the *murran* (warriors) who were sometimes quite belligerent.

The subject came up one evening as we relaxed by the fire digesting one of Daniel's fried steak and cabbage meals, listening to Radio Dar es Salaam play country western songs by Jim Reeves. Finishing his cup of instant coffee, a local Tanganyika product drinkable only with lots of powdered milk, Philip relaxed his lanky frame, crossed an ankle over one knee, and filled his new pipe with another local product, Sweet Nut Tobacco.

"Yas, Dennis, they do sometimes get angry and threaten me, these young *murran*," he admitted. "But I don't care; I just tell them to shut up and listen to their elders." Then he paused a moment to stare irritably at his pipe. "Bugger it!" He had used five matches and it still wouldn't light.

I recommended tamping the tobacco in the pipe bowl to firm it up first, which he did before returning to his story.

"Warriors must fight and protect the cattle of their *boma*, that is true. However, they must also obey their elders. It is our tradition. And, you know what?" he pointed his pipe at me, which was now smoking, "I am an elder! That is why I can own cattle, which *murran* cannot do. Therefore, I force them to answer my questions."

He gazed thoughtfully at the ceiling for a few minutes before speaking again.

"But they probably lie," he admitted, staring in disappointment at his pipe, which had gone out.

In fact, Philip shared the deep aversion of the Maasai toward livestock taxes. One afternoon he and I sat on the grass outside the house, chinning with Solomon ole Saibull, who was soon to replace Henry Fosbrooke as the new conservator. Philip and Solomon, who were discussing the wedding ceremonies of their closely related tribes, the Maasai and Warusha, were doing most of the talking. Although they were speaking English—probably for my benefit—I paid little heed, my attention wandering to a small storm that was muttering and grumbling its way southward along Ngorongoro Crater's west rim. Small storms frequently did this during the long rains, eventually fetching up against Makarut Mountain several miles to our west. They seldom reached us here at Ngorongoro Settlement.

Then I focused once more on the conversation. Something interesting had arisen. As frequently happens when pastoralists get to talking, the topic of cattle came up, and this had reminded Philip of something. He shared it with us.

"My brother was jailed last month," he said.

Solomon, who had been regally reclining on the grass, like a Roman senator at a banquet, quickly sat up, alert.

"Is it!" he remarked, tone and expression clearly indicating a desire for more information.

"Yas, for sure he was in jail," Philip continued. "So were many other herders in Longido District. They forgot to pay their cattle taxes."

"Ehh," intoned Solomon, his face creased with a knowing grin.

Non-payment of the cattle tax was euphemistically known among the Maasai as "forgetting to pay." This was a strategy which, Solomon and

Philip agreed, was widely practiced by herders, occasionally with some success because the local government taxing agencies were not terribly efficient. However, according to Philip, it appeared that "forgetting to pay" had reached such epic proportions in Longido District that it finally forced the district councilors to take action. What they had done was to hire a fleet of *lorries* (trucks), put some native police in them, and order them to drive around the district arresting every herd owner they could find. They found a great number. Delinquent taxpayers were literally hauled to district headquarters by the truckload. The police then kept them there until their relatives paid the taxes either with money or its equivalent in livestock.

Solomon quickly identified with the councilors. "Hah! That is good!" he declared, enthusiastically striking the ground with his fist.

"But, my cattle were in my brother's herd," Philip complained. "He gave up three for taxes."

Solomon was unsympathetic. "Bwana, he should have given ten." Fixing Philip with a fierce gaze, he asked, "How can we *wananchi*, the people of the land, *jenga taifa*—build the nation—if we pay no taxes?"

"Uh ... but—"

"Isn't it!" Solomon demanded.

"But, gosh," yelped Philip. "Three cows?"

Crack! Boom!

Startled, we looked up to find that the storm on the west rim had quite unexpectedly deviated in our direction and would soon be upon us. Even now, the wind was picking up. *Thump!* The storm gave us a second warning. That was enough for us: we ran for the shelter of the porch as torrents of rain roared on the roof and sluiced in comblike streams from the corrugated *mabati* to flatten the grass.

A traditional Maasai warrior or *murrani*. The ball of ostrich feathers on the spear tip shows he has peaceful intentions.

A modern Maasai: Philip ole Sayalel.

A Welcome Visitor

The day after the buffalo fight I decided to sort and index a large pile of aerial photographs of the Ngorongoro Conservation Area while Daniel did the ironing on the living room table. We had no electricity, so he used an old-fashioned iron. It was simply designed: one just opened it up (it was hinged at the back), shoveled in some hot coals from beneath the Tanganyika boiler, refastened the front end, and got down to work

The two of us went about our separate jobs: Daniel getting my clothes nicely pressed and I, having cleared the floor by shoving what little furniture I had against the wall, trying to arrange hundreds of aerial photographs by flight line and photo number. As the gaps and holes in the coverage filled up, I began to see what the Ngorongoro Conservation Area looked like from the air. I was still immersed in them an hour later—they now covered a large part of the living room floor—when crunching gravel and the beep of a horn outside proclaimed the arrival of visitors. Opening the door I found, parked in the driveway, a small blue car containing three passengers and a turbaned Sikh driver. "Some good friends to see you," announced the latter with a grin. Stooping down to look inside, I recognized three female Peace Corps volunteers from our group, two of whom I still might be able to name except that the third was Cathy, the nurse with whom I had been so taken at the Mgulani Salvation Army Camp.

Ohmygosh! Quickly inviting them in, I undid all my work by sweeping the photos on the floor into a jumbled heap in a corner, dragged my few chairs away from the wall, offered everyone seats, and asked Daniel, who had finished the ironing, to make some coffee.

Cathy's friends, a talkative pair, happily took over the conversation. They were just being tourists, they said, and had stopped by to say hello. They were staying at Dhillon Singh's guesthouse and would go down into the crater tomorrow to see the sights. However, they had already had their day's worth of excitement because their car had gone off the road near Lake Manyara and turned on its side. "It's those Sikh drivers," one of them laughed. "They drive like warriors." But now they were here, and wasn't this a wonderful place to be stationed, and they bet that I never tired of seeing that view out my window, and was that why I had never visited them, and wasn't it awful about that Peace Corps teacher in Singida who was accused of murdering his…?

I hardly heard them. Cathy was even more attractive than I remembered. Trying not to stare, I took in her brown eyes, high cheekbones, and feminine curves. Why, I berated myself, hadn't I become better acquainted with her in Dar es Salaam? Well, she was here now, sitting quietly only a few feet away. Maybe if I—

"Cathy, give Dennis a poke will you," a voice was saying. "He's daydreaming."

"Sorry, I'm just tired, that's all. Didn't sleep well last night." I told them about the buffaloes fighting outside my room.

"Oh, you get all the fun don't you," joshed the one who had enjoyed the car accident.

"That's all right," said her companion. "We were about to go anyway."

Nononono, not yet! I have to do something about Cathy! "Look around outside first," I quickly suggested. "The view's better in front. You might see some wildlife."

So we went outside and somehow Cathy lingered with me while the others wandered off. Sternly instructing myself to connect (tell her she's cute, ask her for dinner, do *something*!), I took the plunge. "Cathy would you.... " Gulping for air like a fish in the bottom of an angler's boat, I fell silent—*she was standing so close!* I didn't know what to say, so I just babbled: about the ecology of Ngorongoro Crater, what I did all day, my colleagues' amusing adventures, Daniel's marital problems....

Suddenly Cathy looked up at me with distracting brown eyes and said, "Dennis, I've been thinking about you a lot lately." Then, she serenely turned to the view of Ngorongoro Crater, leaving me gulping like a fish again.

But she had given me the courage I needed. When next I was able to speak, I invited her to dinner at the lodge.

"Why, that would be nice, I'd like that," she replied, smiting me with a knee-wobbling smile.

Only after everyone had said their goodbyes and disappeared up the driveway did gray-garbed Reality grab my innards with a steely grip and ask how I planned to pick Cathy up—Dhillon Singh's guesthouse was three buffalo- and elephant-infested miles away and I had no transport.

Well, that did it. I had been elated; now I was dejected. Turning toward the house, I thought of Shakespeare's Richard III who, finding himself in a tight spot, had cried out, "My kingdom for a horse!" He had my sympathy. Right now I would trade all I owned (a 35 mm camera, several dog-eared paperback books, and two changes of clothes), for something with wheels and an engine.

Then I noticed the Land Rover parked in front of John Goddard's house.

The door to the Goddard's house was open, so I announced my presence with a loud "*Hodi?*" and entered without waiting for someone to say "*Karibu.*" (We were easy neighbors.) John was sitting at the living room table, looking at 35 mm colored slides with a hand-held slide viewer. He removed a slide from the viewer and tossed it onto the floor where forty or fifty others lay in a loose pile. I couldn't believe what he was doing—color transparencies were expensive.

"Are those rejects on the floor? Where are the good ones?"

John silently pointed to several slides on the table in front of him. Then he threw another slide on the floor. Any other time, I would have searched through the pile for some to keep, but not now.

"John, can I borrow your car tonight?"

"Why, you got a date?" Amused at the thought, he placed a slide on the "keep" pile.

"Yes."

For the first time, he looked up: "You serious?"

I explained about my visitors, that I had invited one of them to the lodge tonight but needed a car.

"Shelly! *Shelly!* Come and hear this!"

Wearing her usual jeans and bulky long-sleeved sweater, Shelly padded into the living room in stocking feet, a book in one hand and a *this had better be good* expression on her face. Penny trailed along behind.

"Guess who has a date."

Shelly's eyes widened in amazement; then they narrowed and twinkled.

"It's about time! Well, come on, what's her name? Was she in the car that just went out?"

I described Cathy

"You're kidding; you mean the pretty one?" (John had paid more attention to my visitors than he'd been letting on.)

I admitted that I thought so, and asked again—well, *some* people might have called it pleading—for the Land Rover.

"Sorry," he replied, trying to keep a straight face. "I'm going out tonight to look for rhinos."

"But, you promised to play *Snakes and Ladders* with me tonight, Daddy. You promised!" Penny wailed. She was only four. Her mother frowned.

"Just hand over the keys," she told her husband. "Dennis needs to muck the car out before his date."

The main lodge building, with its pillar wood walls and decorative bamboo partitions between beams and roof, was attractively rustic. The dining area was a large room with a stone fireplace at one end, a bar at the other, and maybe a dozen tables in between. Large picture windows, curtained now that night had fallen, extended along the north face of the lodge where it looked out over the crater. The safari suits worn by some of the diners contributed to the ambience. One of them had a vest with canvas bullet holders sewn to its front.

Over dinner Cathy and I became better acquainted. At first rather reticent about herself, she gradually opened up and talked about Philadelphia, where she had grown up in a neighborhood of small row houses with tiny front yards. Kids played in the streets; people rode buses and patronized family-owned bakeries, grocery shops, and bars within walking distance of their homes. City garbage collectors loudly banged metal refuse cans about, and tradesmen, called hucksters, passed up and down the streets selling ice cream, ears of sweet corn fresh from the fields, and housewares from their carts and trucks. During the hot, humid summers, families escaped the city to rent rooms and houses at the Jersey shore, sometimes for a month or more, while the fathers stayed behind and visited them on weekends. The less fortunate spent muggy summer evenings on their tiny porches fanning themselves and talking with their neighbors. Cathy had never attended a public school.

She and her older sister and brother went to Catholic schools where black-robed nuns administered strict discipline and made everyone attend mass (even her nursing college had been Catholic). It sounded so different from my own experiences growing up in a small town in the West that Philadelphia could have been a foreign country.

After eating we moved to a smaller table closer to the bar to have our coffee. Relaxing, we lit up, Cathy effortlessly lighting her cigarettes with a chrome-plated lighter while I labored away at firing up my pipe with box after box of poor quality stick matches. They broke during striking, or they didn't strike at all, or they fizzed without flaming, or they exploded into a flame that singed my eyebrows. Then, after the pipe was lit, I had to keep attending to it because it kept dying. But Cathy didn't seem bothered. Indeed, she regarded my pipe maintenance activities with what looked suspiciously like amusement. The conversation flowed, to the extent that only a few minutes seemed to have passed when Cathy looked at her watch and exclaimed at how late it was. She had to get back.

Reluctantly I paid the bill, and we left. The Maasai guard rose to his feet as we went outside but sat down again upon learning that we were not staying at the lodge. We wouldn't need him and his spear to escort us past grazing buffaloes to our cabin. On the drive back to Dhillon Singh's place, I showed off by identifying animals along the road from the reflection of their eyes in the car's headlights. Looking to see if Cathy was impressed, I found her regarding me wonderingly: clearly, my expertise had moved her. All these years she'd been waiting for someone who could identify animals by shining lights in their eyes—and now here he was! She'd be feeling my muscles next. Touching my arm, she softly spoke.

"Dennis?"

"Mmm?"

"Do you read the *Economist*?"

Two mornings later the small blue car once again crunched to a halt outside my house. This time Cathy's friends, under the pretext of photographing some flowers farther up the driveway, left us alone for a few, exceedingly short minutes. Time enough, however, to confirm that we wanted to continue seeing each other. Then, just before leaving, Cathy surprised me with the gift of her cigarette lighter. She laughed: "You need it more than I do."

Cathy's friends soon returned to collect her. Leaning out of the window, Cathy called out, "Don't forget to write!" Then the car turned a corner and she was gone. For some minutes I stared into the distance with unfocused eyes before a gust of cool air whipping across the yard returned me to the present. Entering the house, I stared out the window for a while longer, lost in thought. But then I snapped out of it. Rummaging out a piece of paper, I began to write a letter:

Dear Cathy …

Cathy Lange.

Forest Patrols and Grass Fires

Bee Hives and Elephant Trails

The morning was misty and cool. Just the right level of cool, too, although I would have welcomed more sunshine. The Africans of our little community on the rim of Ngorongoro Crater probably would have preferred a lot more sunshine. I deduced this from the extra blankets, sweaters and coats everyone was wearing; one gentleman had a greatcoat with fur collar that seemed more appropriate to wintertime in Minnesota.

I was going on safari today, to visit one of the forest guards stationed along the lower (southern) edge of the Northern Highlands Forest Reserve. I wanted to see how clearly the boundary of the forest reserve was marked and learn about the problems he faced. I also wanted to give him moral support. I felt he probably needed it because, like game scouts, most forest guards lived and worked miles away from headquarters, had no transport, limited supervision, and often came under strong pressure from the people they lived among to overlook or bend forest regulations. Unlike game scouts, they were unarmed.

The primary purposes of the Northern Highlands Reserve were to produce water and provide habitat for wildlife. The forest moderated the microenvironment, stabilized the soil, condensed precipitation from fog, and expedited the infiltration of rainfall into the soil, thereby providing a steady supply of water throughout the year. The thirty or more springs and streams originating within the forest were either tapped or flowed outside the reserve to benefit coffee estates, Wambulu villages, and Maasai livestock. Some of the streams flowed over the escarpment where they helped maintain highly important groundwater forest habitat in Lake Manyara National Park. The forest also provided cover and food for wildlife, the most notable being rhinoceros, elephant, and buffalo. Indeed, the latter two species were seen there more often than in the crater. John Goddard thought that many of the rhinos in the crater also lived in the forest and Henry Fosbrooke was convinced that the forest provided seasonal habitat for elephants from Lake Manyara National Park.

In fact, Henry, who was still conservator at the time, had spoken to me on that very subject earlier in the morning. He came out of his office just as I was about to enter mine so our conversation took place in the grassy "courtyard" between the two single-story red *mabati*-roofed buildings—one cement block, the other wooden—that comprised the offices of the Ngorongoro Conservation Unit.

"Dennis, I have a re—"

"*Arusha, Arusha, Arusha, this is Ngorongoro, Ngorongoro, Ngorongoro. Come in Arusha, Arusha, Arusha. Arusha, Arusha, Arusha, this is....*"

Loud voices exploded from the single-room police station in the cement block building. The constables were calling headquarters in Arusha by short wave radio. The radio loudly crackled, whined and blared in reply. Raising his voice so that I could hear, Henry continued.

He was concerned that new farms were about to block the only remaining elephant trail connecting the Northern Highlands Forest Reserve with Lake Manyara National Park. Encouraged by the territorial government, people had been moving onto land south of the forest reserve for some twenty years. A new government-sponsored settlement scheme presently was expanding into one of the last remaining pieces of unoccupied land near Kitete Village. The elephant trail passed through this area so Henry felt it was just a matter of time before it was plowed under for crops.

Where they could, he explained, elephants in East Africa habitually moved to highland forests to obtain forage, water, and shade during the dry season, then moved back onto lower elevation rangelands after rainfall had turned the vegetation green and filled the seasonal streams and waterholes. However, an expanding human population was taking more and more land for settlements and farms that blocked the old elephant migration routes. Consequently, some elephant populations were in danger of being bottled up within their dry season forest habitats and, eventually, destroying them. Henry didn't want that to happen here so he meant to protect the trail near Kitete Village by persuading the government to gazette it as part of the Ngorongoro Conservation Area. For political reasons, this would be a difficult task but it would be even harder once farms occupied the site.

"So, while you're at the forest guard station, walk over and have a look will you? The trail is nearby."

With that, Henry turned to greet a Maasai *murrani* who had been leaning on his spear a few feet away, curiously watching, and then hurried busily away.

As often happened, the major hurdle of the day was actually getting on the road. First, I had to discuss some business with forest officers Mlangai and Peter: someone had to oversee the cutting of a truckload of bamboo ordered by Richard Leaky for use at the archeological dig at Oldupai Gorge; grass growing beneath the electric fence surrounding the eucalyptus plantation had to be cut or it would short out the electricity; tree seedlings growing in polythene tubes in the nursery needed shifting so they wouldn't root in the soil below. Then I discovered that my gas lantern wasn't working and had to search around for a wrench to adjust it. By the time the Land Rover finally arrived, an hour late, I had also found I had no *panga* for the safari so I took the car to the storehouse at Mili Tatu (so-named because it was three miles away) to get one. Returning to the office, I signed some letters. Afterward, I bought some food for the trip—mostly tins of Chinese fruit cocktail and corned beef—at the local *duka*. Then we finally set out, only to stop again at the Kampi ya Nyoka (Lodoare) gate, fourteen miles down the road, so the driver could buy cigarettes and another eight miles farther on, at Karatu, so I could buy some bread.

After Karatu, we turned onto a dirt road that passed through the settlement scheme Henry was worried about. Called the Upper Kitete Village Settlement Scheme, it was settling people of the Wambulu tribe on previously uncultivated land and teaching them new, improved methods of agriculture. Each farmer had three acres for his personal use, but all members, using tractors and combines, helped to farm the larger area of common land and took equal shares of the profits. I noticed several farmers walking along the road with heavy, broad-bladed hoes over their shoulders. Farther away, two or three tractors were busily plowing the fields.

Nicolas, the forest guard I was visiting, patrolled a twelve-mile stretch of boundary from near Mbulumbulu Village east to the Selela River. He and his porter, Malchias, lived by themselves in a small guard station near Kitete Village. It was a standard government outstation structure: twenty by twenty feet, wooden walls with exposed studs, and *mabati* roof. It had four rooms, unglazed windows with wooden shutters, and plank beds. One room, blackened by smoke, had been converted into a kitchen by building a fire on the concrete floor. Smoke vented out the window and through spaces between the walls and roof. Nicolas and Malchias were both married and had large families, but they lived like bachelors because their families were in Mbulu Town, fifty miles away. If they were lucky, they got home for a day or two maybe once a month.

The driver dropped me off and drove back to Ngorongoro where someone else would use the Land Rover while I was away. He would return in three days to pick me up. I pitched my tent on the grass and spent the rest of the day getting to know the men.

Next morning Nicolas donned a long-sleeved sweater and a green beret to which was pinned his official forest department badge. Then he and Malchias, who had neither sweater nor cap, took me west along the forest reserve boundary. The forest resembled a dark green landslide that had stopped just short of the boundary line. Fingers of trees extended beyond the boundary; but they were doomed: soon they would be cleared and turned into farmland. Gaps in the foliage, variously shaped tree crowns, and an occasional tree standing above the others roughly textured the canopy. A fringe of vines, shrubs and small trees tapered and softened the forest's edge. Here and there, widely scattered cordia and Cape chestnut trees bloomed; their showy masses of white and pinkish flowers standing out against the dark vegetation.

We followed the boundary, which was well marked, as far as Mbulumbulu Village and the coffee plantations. Indeed, the boundary would have been hard to miss as it was a twelve-foot wide band of bare soil that had been cleared with hoes just last year (I had seen worse looking roads). No trespasser could say he hadn't seen *this* boundary. It also was wide enough to be a good firebreak.

With the boundary off my mind, we entered the forest. Except where sunlight leaked through the overhead foliage to lightly speckle the forest floor, it was pleasingly dim—the bright sunlight outside had made me squint. Walking on soft leaf litter, we pushed our way through an often dense under-story of shrubs, small trees and occasional lianas. Then Nicolas stopped and made a sweeping gesture.

"*Miti mkubwa!*" Big trees, he exclaimed, showing off a bit.

All around us, pillar woods with smooth, silvery boles, olives with steeply ascendant branches, and flat-topped crotons and albizias, rose sixty to a hundred feet into the air, their lower parts partially screened by under-story vegetation. Many were straight and free of branches almost to the canopy. Some bore epiphytic orchids and ferns on their branches.

Well, I didn't think the trees *that* big: I'd worked with larger ones, some so big that several people had to join hands to circle their circumference. But I hadn't yet seen a forest I didn't like and this was no exception. It was peaceful here. Only occasionally did the ringing call of a bird, or the rustling of a small animal rooting among fallen leaves disturb the forest's stillness. It was a place both private and welcoming.

The forest also intrigued me because I knew so little about it. For instance, what was that large tree next to Malchias with smooth gray bark dotted with light pink patches? Pygeum? Fagaropsis? Ekebergia? And I hadn't a clue about the under-story shrubs. Luckily, Nicolas and Malchias were able to name them for me in Kimbulu, their tribal language. I wrote the names down, hoping to match them with scientific names in a reference book, *Kenya Trees and Shrubs,* bought on my last trip to Arusha.

At 2 p.m., the end of the official seven hour working day (with half a day on Saturday), Nicolas and Malchias went home. Instead of accompanying them, I walked over to the settlement scheme where I found the expatriate managers having tea on a shady porch. They politely provided a chair and cup and we spent the next hour talking business, griping, and telling amusing stories. One topic was the new houses the scheme was building for its farmers, each with a concrete floor, metal frame, and *mabati* roof, but no walls. The idea, said Nick, the English manager, was to entice the farmers from their old-fashioned, mud and thatch huts into more modern, spacious, and healthier housing. All the farmers had to do was to add the walls themselves and they could move in.

However, few were doing it, and Nick thought he knew why.

Granted, he said, the farmers were a conservative bunch, but they also knew the new *mabati*-roofed houses to be uncomfortably hot in warm weather. He had anticipated resistance on this issue but his bosses in Dar es Salaam had definite ideas about what constituted d*evelopment,* and they wanted modern buildings.

Next morning, after drinking our breakfast tea, Nicolas, Malchias and I set out to patrol the forest reserve boundary on the other side of the guard station. Leaving behind the large fields, tractors, roads, and corrugated tin roofs of the settlement scheme we entered a different world. Here, small homesteads of cylindrical mud huts with conical grass-thatch roofs, small gardens, and occasional clumps of banana trees dotted rolling grassland. Smoke from cooking fires rose into the air. Scattered herds of cattle grazed under the eyes of herd boys. From the forest's edge, we looked across undulating grassland to where the escarpment abruptly fell away, two thousand feet to the Maasai Steppe. Mantled by dry grass peppered with outcrops of black lava, the steppe disappeared eastward into the already thickening haze. To the north and northeast, their outlines softened by the haze, volcanic peaks with Maasai names—Kerimasi, Oldoinyo Lengai, Kitumbeine—rose high above the steppe.

This looked so much like my vision of old Africa that it was easy to imagine its having been like this forever (only later did I learn that the people here were recent settlers). I even went to the trouble of unbuttoning my heavy thirty-five mm camera and spending several minutes fiddling about with shutter speeds, f-stops, and focusing—always a frustrating procedure for me—in order to click off several photographs. What a place to live, I thought, so tranquil and scenic; the people here must be a contented lot. "Who are these lucky folk?" I exclaimed.

"They are Warusha," Nicolas replied. "They are bad people!"

"Yes, yes, very bad!" agreed Malchias.

"They say if we keep their *ng'ombe* (cattle) from forest they will beat us!"

"Kill us!" corrected Malchias with raised voice. "They are cruel people!"

Yes, well; so much for my imaginings. But not an illogical response considering that the Wambulu and the Warusha/Maasai were traditional enemies, or at best, mutually wary neighbors. However, it did set me wondering about how effective Nicolas and Malchias might be in protecting their part of the forest reserve.

We continued onward, occasionally diverting into the forest reserve itself whenever Nicolas and Malchias had hard evidence to show me of illegal activities by the Warusha. We found trails littered with bovine droppings that the two men assured me were those of cattle rather than buffalo. Here and there, a tree had been felled and part of it removed. (I learned that the bark of one such tree was a medicinal ingredient.) Scattered about were beehives. Now these in no way resembled the boxes that farmers use as beehives back home. Instead, they were sections of tree trunks, about five or six feet long and maybe a foot and a half in diameter, which had been split lengthwise, hollowed out, wired back together again and then either hung from or placed in the branches of a tree. The bees built their hives within the hollowed logs. Periodically, a hive's owner built a fire beneath it to give the bees a good smoking so that he could climb up and remove the honey from the log. Unfortunately, the fire sometimes escaped and spread into the surrounding forest, which was one reason why the location of the hives had to be regulated. The other reason was that a good-sized tree had to be cut down to make the hive in the first place and this was all too often done right on-site in the forest.

Several times we noticed herds of cattle grazing near the boundary or being driven swiftly away from it by herd boys with sharp whistles and vigorous whacks of sturdy sticks. Each time, Nicolas and Malchias quickly ran ahead and searched the bare soil of the hoed boundary line for hoof prints or cowpats—evidence of trespass. They never found any so we kept walking. The cattle were rather small, grayish animals with distinctive humps, like those on Brahman bulls at rodeos. "Zebus," said Nicolas. A few had strangely bent horns which my two companions told me were made that way by the herdsmen, who felt it added to their cattle's beauty and desirability. Some of the bulls bore the brands of ownership: single straight lines, several parallel lines, circles, crosses—one animal carried a shallowly angled chevron scar along much of the length of its body. These too, Nicolas and Malchias assured me, were beauty marks as well as ownership brands.

We crossed several rivers along the way. Nicolas named some of them for me: Kitete, Losetete, Nagangalo. Small, cloudy streams, three to fifteen feet wide and usually less than a foot deep, they emerged from the cool, shadowed tangles of the forest to warm themselves for a few miles, flowing through shallow valleys in the open grassland, before tumbling over the edge of the escarpment. One little stream with no name bashfully seeped away into the ground part way there. Sometime in the early afternoon, we came to the Selela River and there we had to stop because we found our way blocked by a deep canyon that might have been chopped into the landscape by a celestial meat cleaver. Its steep walls, at least a thousand feet deep, were cloaked with a dense growth of vines, creepers and shrubs from which emerged a scattering of large fire-resistant euphorbia trees with sturdy candelabrum-like branches. On the far slope was the black scar of a recent fire. Elsewhere, relict trees and dead snags stood above the creepers and shrubs. Fires sweeping up the steep slopes had destroyed the original forest.

Two swifts audibly *whished* overhead, dove deeply into the canyon and then out again like hot-shot pilots at an air show. They quickly passed out of sight. Somewhere behind us a wooden cowbell clunked. The two forest officers quickly swiveled to see if they could tell which side of the forest boundary it had come from. I returned to the practicalities of life.

"So, Nicolas, where do we cross?" I asked.

"Oh, Mr. Dinnis, we do not cross," he replied in surprise.

From here on, he said, there was no cleared forest boundary. Neither was there any patrolling; never had been to his knowledge. It was, indeed, possible to cross the Selela River, but whoever took the trouble would arrive hours later on the other side only to find three more canyons lying in wait over the next ten miles. And the area was full of elephant and buffalo.

"Tunaogopa wanyama," Nicolas confessed. We fear the animals.

"Kweli!" agreed Malchias, getting excited again. *"Hatutaki kufa!"* We do not want to die!

Roughly half of the entire forest reserve—that part of it northeast of the Selela River (about thirty linear miles of boundary)—was unpatrolled and unprotected.

Back at the forest guard's house, we rested. Several people, some wearing Muslim *kofias* (skull caps), had walked over from the settlement scheme to sprawl on the lawn and pass the time of day. Nicolas, who, now that the work day was over, was clad in a colorful red and gold saronglike garment called a *kikoi*, read some government circulars to them which had been written in Swahili. He did this because some of the visitors were illiterate. But because African culture is oral rather than literary, even those who could read and write were willing to listen and comment—they really did enjoy talking, no matter who was doing it. Anyway, the group listened attentively, now and then erupting into discussion over some piece of news.

Noticing the gathering, the headman of the local Warusha, a tall, stately man dressed in black pants and a cream-colored jacket with narrow lapels, stopped to exchange greetings and see what was going on.

"Jambo mzee." Hello, old man. Nicolas greeted him. *"Karibu."*

Welcome (literally: come near). Bringing two wobbly wooden chairs from the house, he politely seated his visitor on one before taking the other. He wanted to speak with the headman.

"*Habari za nyumbani?*" How is your house?

"*Nzuri. Habari za hapa.*" It is good. How is it here?

"*Nzuri. Habari ya ng'ombe?*" Good. How are your cattle?

There were two or three more exchanges before Nicolas could get down to business:

"*Mzee, iko shida,*" he said. Old man, there is a problem.

Nicolas told the headman about the difficulties he and Malchias were having with the Warusha, especially over beehives. He explained why these were illegal within the forest reserve and must be removed. The *mzee* listened; periodically interjecting attentive "ehhhhhh's" and "*kweli's*" (Swahili for true) but otherwise was silent until the flow of Nicolas's words had run its course.

When it came his turn to speak, he replied in English, pausing between sentences for maximum effect. Pointing his yard-long *fimbo* (a sort of swagger stick) in the direction of the Warusha settlements, he said, "Bwana Nicolas, my people are bullheaded. They agree with everything I tell them. But, then they do what they want." Then, leaning forward on his *fimbo*, which elicited a protesting squeak from his chair, he took Nicolas into his confidence: "What can one do with such people?" he asked.

Then the *mzee* heaved himself to his feet and with a regal smile continued on his way. As I watched him stride off, two thoughts occurred to me. The first was that both men had really been talking more to me than to each other; the second was that the headman probably had beehives in the forest himself, the old scoundrel.

The next morning we woke to find ourselves blanketed by a warm, damp fog. We would have felt isolated and lonely except for the clear ringing clangs of the primary school's "bell"—an old truck wheel rim strung on a rope between two upright posts—being vigorously rung with a broken tire iron across the Losetete River. Even now, youngsters in green uniforms would be groping their way to school. We ourselves soon set out through the mist, but in the opposite direction.

"There it is, Bwana Dinnis", said Nicolas as we topped the hill. "*Njia ya tembo.*" Trail of the elephants. We were near the edge of the escarpment a few miles southwest of the guard station. Visibility was good because we emerged from the fog soon after starting out. I forgot about the seven waterbucks spotted a few minutes earlier and turned my attention to the two wide paths—each probably hundreds of years old or more—that passed on opposite sides of the hill and crossed the grassy slope before us. "*Mashamba huko pale.*" Nicolas exclaimed. There are farms there. Where the two trails once converged before descending the escarpment, there were now fields belonging to the settlement scheme. The conservator's difficulties had just significantly increased.

Afterward, I walked from the guard station to a grassy hill near the forest edge. Worried about the effectiveness of the forest guards, the poor protection that much of the forest reserve was receiving, the blocking by cultivated fields of the major elephant trail down the escarpment, (and whether my ride back to Ngorongoro would be late), I wanted to think. But the warm sunshine and soft caresses of a breeze that was furrowing and ruffling the grass soon had their effect. I began to relax. A small buck quietly emerged from the forest to graze, pausing now and then to check on me. A hornbill sounded off, loud and brassy, from inside a narrow finger of forest at the bottom of a nearby valley. Warbling larks flitted here and there above the grass and scattered orange gladioli. My concerns dropped away. I would take them up later—maybe.

Hamisi, the driver arrived to pick me up at 5 p.m. just as he had promised. For a short time I had hopes of getting home in time for a hot bath and a warm meal. But as is the way in the African bush where supplies are scattered, transport scarce, and demand high, we spent hours driving here and there picking up gunny sacks of maize flour, charcoal, vegetables, and fruit for people back at Ngorongoro. We took money to someone's sick relative, dropped off another somebody's nephew at his school, picked up yet another person's aunt to take back with us to Ngorongoro, and gave rides to people along the road. We also changed a flat tire, and filled up with gas. Furthermore, this being Africa, each stop was an opportunity to socialize: twice, we were invited to tea. So it was that we finally reached Ngorongoro at ten p.m., five hours after setting out, by which time Daniel had retired to bed and the water in the Tanganyika boiler had cooled to lukewarm. I splashed tepid water over my head to remove some of the dust, ate a cold dinner straight from the tin, and went to bed. Hot food and water would have to wait until tomorrow.

Trespassers in the Forest

A new month had begun, bringing with it a renewed fuel ration for the Land Rover. It was time to sort out those herders who were trespassing in the forest. A recent flight in a small plane over the Northern Highlands Forest Reserve revealed that the pessimistic views of the Kitete guards were not pessimistic enough. From the air I saw illegal *bomas*, many herds of cattle, and multiple acres blackened by fires set by herders and honey gatherers. This was unacceptable. The local people were acting as though the forest reserve didn't exist. Something had to be done.

Therefore, on the third day of the month, I took several forest guards and game scouts twenty miles or so to a place near Lemala where they said we would find *"Ng'ombe ningi sana."* Very many cattle. And they were right. Parking the car, we made our way through a screen of shrubs, and found a herd in the very first grassy glade. We arrested the herdsmen.

They were indignant. "Reserve? We are not in reserve! Boundary? We saw no boundary. Oh that! But that is old boundary. Anyway, it is drought and we always come here in drought. Whose authority? Bwana Steff-son (a former District Officer named Steve Stephenson).

Gone? When? That long ago? Oh. But look, we have permit. Yes, look here!" The herder quickly extracted a paper from an aluminum 35 mm film canister in a large hole in his ear lobe. But its contents, *Mto wa Mbu Grocery, Naranjan Singh, Proprietor, 2 lbs. sugar, 16 shillings,* failed to move our icy hearts. The herders were taken aback. They had felt this grocery receipt to be as potentially powerful as other documents (titles, Local Purchase Orders, deeds, permits) they had seen in government offices. It was paper with writing on it.

Our catch that day totaled four Maasai and about a thousand cattle, which is a lot of stock to be trampling about in a protected forest reserve, even one this size. The forest guards duly rounded up the cattle and herded them off to Ngorongoro. The herdsmen, now prisoners, had to come with us so they couldn't escape. However, judging from the grins on their faces and the enthusiasm with which they pointed out the sights along the way, they didn't want to. Being in the clutches of the law didn't seem to worry them at all.

Two days later, I accompanied more forest guards and game scouts on a foray deep into the forest reserve. Beginning near Kitete Village, we walked through quiet, shadowy forest where a layer of fallen leaves in various stages of decay gave the forest floor a soft and springy feel. But soon we found ourselves in more-open scrubby vegetation with little shade and hard ground supporting patches of heavily grazed, stubby grass. All that remained of the original forest were scattered groups of trees and numerous stumps. Fire and livestock had done their damage.

Now we began to see signs that livestock were in the area, i.e., trails littered with cow dung and a recently abandoned cattle *boma* or enclosure. The trails became more numerous and well-defined as we progressed deeper into the reserve. Some were so wide you could drive a car down them. We had come to the right place, all right.

We were an odd-looking bunch. Each of the men wore his own unique version of forest guard or game scout uniform, while I sported a red felt deer-hunting hat that I had brought with me from the States. Our weapons were equally varied—standard issue Lee Enfield .303 rifles for the two game scouts, and an ancient shotgun, long spear, and two *pangas* for the usually unarmed forest guards. I carried no weapon. We looked more like a ragtag army of deserters out to loot and pillage than official enforcers of the law. Carefully, we filed down first one then another hard-packed cattle trail, looking for trespassing herders and their cattle.

Suddenly ahead, a soft *clunk* sounded. We exchanged knowing looks and grins. That was a wooden cowbell. The chief forest guard, an older man whose stiff curly hair was sprinkled with white, whispered that we should be especially quiet now. Easing our way slowly around stumps, we carefully pushed branches aside to look ahead, studying each clearing before entering it, tense with anticipation.

At least the others did. A few hundred feet down the trail I was distracted by a bluish green bird flashing through the shrubbery. Lilac breasted roller?

"*Wewe! Simama!*" You there! Stop!

"*Kamata yeye!*" Catch him!

Guards and scouts alike charged into the bushes from which they emerged a few minutes later, triumphantly pushing before them a young Maasai herd boy. But, he wasn't a talkative herd boy. When questioned about who he was and why he was here, he just grinned cheekily and refused to say a word. I was irritated but my men took it in stride—Africans are remarkably easygoing and tolerant of naughty youngsters—and merely warned him not to escape. He joined our party willingly enough, and we continued on our way.

Cattle began to appear along the trail and among the shrubs, but we decided not to round any up yet. We would first try to catch more herders. This time I tried to stay alert. And for about two minutes I was, before being distracted by the aerial roots of a strangler fig hanging from a tree branch just off the trail. Now, *this* was interesting. I stepped over to have a quick look. They were the *strangest* looking things. If you overlooked the absence of suckers, the fig's aerial roots resembled the tentacles of a large dead octopus hanging limply from the branches. Some years earlier, a bird high in the tree had eaten a fig. A seed from the fig, instead of falling to the ground had come to rest (most likely) in the fork between the trunk and a large branch. The seed had germinated and grown into an epiphytic bush living on moisture and nutrients from cracks and hollows in the tree where rainfall and debris collected, or from decaying leaves caught up in its own roots. It had sent down aerial roots, some creeping down the trunk of the host tree, others, like those in front of me—tipped with little brushes of reddish rootlets—descending vertically through the air. Once rooted in the soil the roots would multiply, branch, and join together, encasing the host tree in a woody mesh. Eventually, the host tree would die, due to physical constriction by the enlarging fig tree perhaps, or shading from its expanding foliage, or competition from its roots. I had seen an advanced case of this once and it was a marvelous sight: a big strangler fig with its dead and decaying host—itself a large tree—still clutched tightly in its embrace.

I was alone. My companions had vanished. Hurrying in what I hoped was the right direction I found them in the next clearing clustered around a Maasai *murrani*. Clad in a blanket against the early morning chill, the herder had been leaning on his spear looking the other direction and chewing, of all things, on a honey comb. He had been so unaware of our presence that the guards had simply walked up and surrounded him. Maasai *murran* made a point of being unimpressed by anything, but this one had been briefly startled. We were the last thing he'd expected to encounter here deep in the forest.

"Cattle? What cattle?"

Plop, a cow softly defecated a few feet away. A loud bovine bellow rattled the bushes. Three steers trotted across the trail near the edge of the clearing.

"Oh, those cattle; I'm just passing through so I know nothing about them. Maybe they are Wambulu cattle."

He continued in this vein for several minutes before admitting he recognized the cattle. Their owner, he assured us, would be angry to hear that the herd boys had brought his animals into the forest. Pointing his chin at our young prisoner, he said, "I will take him and the cattle to his father who will punish him severely."

But the chief forest officer had heard enough. "*Wacha mpuzi wewe!*" Leave this foolishness, you!" he said and confiscated the *murrani*'s spear.

The warrior just grinned. "*Nipe cigara*" he said. Give me a cigarette.

Leaving one of the game scouts behind to guard the prisoners, we continued our search. As we walked away the two captives and the scout hunkered down on their heels in the shade of a large bush, the *murrani* smoking the cigarette he had bummed, bantering away like old friends.

That day we netted six people, over a thousand cattle, and almost certainly missed many more. Counting the ones taken near Lemala, we had caught over two thousand cattle in two days, which made me wonder if there weren't more livestock inside the forest reserve than out. No wonder the forest was so degraded. Of the six people we caught, the chief forest guard detained two and let the other four go, having made them promise to present themselves at the Magistrate's Court at Karatu on the appropriate day.

"But how do you know they will turn up?" I asked.

"Don't worry, bwana, we know them. The other two we do not know. Besides, we have their cattle. They will come." (They did too.)

Three days later, nineteen people piled into two Land Rovers for the drive from Ngorongoro to the Magistrate's Court at Karatu, thirty miles away. The group included six people to be tried; Conservation Unit staff members (including me and the forest guards) who were to give evidence; drivers; policemen; Dhillon Singh, the manager of the Forest Resort, who had caught one of his employees stealing; and six relatives who just needed a lift. The springs of the Land Rovers were dangerously flat.

The two Maasai we caught near Lemala hadn't lost their enthusiasm for tourism, especially after we left the forest reserve and started across the Mbulu Plateau. This was new country to them. But, they hastened to explain, previous generations of warriors had certainly come this way, for Maasai *murran* once raided cattle far and wide until the better-armed *wazungu* (Europeans) appeared and put a stop to it. One prisoner's grandfather had almost died near here about seventy years earlier when a nighttime cattle raid failed. He escaped only by painfully squeezing into a hyena den where he lay, dirt dribbling down the back of his neck, and animal noises emanating from somewhere under his feet, while an army of Wambulu warriors raged about overhead searching for him. Luckily, they didn't poke a torch down his particular hole.

The Magistrate's Court was a single-room building about twenty by forty-five feet, with a concrete floor and raised concrete platform at one end where the magistrate sat, a dignified-looking African in his late thirties. Everyone else—accused, accusers, onlookers—sat on benches arranged in a single row around the perimeter of the room. Thanks to the crowd from Ngorongoro, the room was overflowing that day. Wedged tightly into a row of bodies occupying one of the benches, I waited my turn to give evidence—a long wait as it turned out.

The proceedings, conducted in a quiet monotone, were mostly in Swahili, which I still had difficulty following. And the day was warm. A large bluebottle fly buzzed fruitlessly against a dirty windowpane. Swallows swooped just outside the window, returning to mud-daubed nests under the eaves to feed their young (I could hear the nestlings cheeping). A small black spider rappelled toward the floor from a dusty rafter; once it reached the floor, it stood an excellent chance of being stepped on. On the far wall, a flesh-colored, large-eyed gecko stalked a fly in intermittent short, wiggly dashes, with such long pauses in between that I thought the fly would think of something else to do and fly away before the gecko got there.

Spectators came and went. A Maasai *mzee* had an interesting-looking cow horn container hanging from a leather thong around his neck. I wondered what he carried in it. Snuff? Tobacco? Medicine? Two young boys sitting with their gum booted father stared at me in wonder. "*Mzungu*," they exclaimed softly. White man. I was a novelty. A small bird had flown in through the open door; now it fluttered overhead—too high to find the door—peeping in alarm as it tried to get out again. A young Mbulu mother, wearing a dress made of green *kitenge* cloth stamped with a design of black pineapples, exposed her breast to nurse her baby. I quickly looked away.

The proceedings droned on. The spider yo-yoed up and down its thread most of the morning. Every time it reached the floor a nearby movement made it scuttle rapidly back up again. Finally it gave up and retreated to the rafter. Around midmorning the bluebottle fly abruptly stopped buzzing, snapped up by the gecko, which celebrated its meal with vigorous bobs of its head. Half-an-hour later, the fluttering bird blundered through the open door to gain its freedom. Outside, the swallows continued to swoop, and their nestlings to cheep.

Finally the magistrate decided to take up the Ngorongoro cases and the forest guards and I gave my testimony. But, he wasn't interested. He scarcely listened. He asked no questions. It was all over in a few minutes. Now I knew why he had left us until last.

The magistrate gave the trespassers a stern lecture about misusing precious natural resources; but it was mere form. Then he levied such a laughably small fine that it was paid on the spot by a relative of the defendants. This elder was not poor either. He peeled the few bills needed for the fine from a roll of money the size of a large hand grenade. And that was that.

"They treat these fines as grazing fees" whispered Solomon ole Saibull into my ear. He was here to give evidence in one of the cases. "They would willingly pay even greater amounts." Keeping his voice low, he told me that in his experience African magistrates seldom imposed heavy fines for forest trespass because they didn't think it was a very important offense. Most Africans, educated or not, considered forest reserves to be relics of colonialism, set aside by the *wazungu* for their own purposes, not the African's. "He [the magistrate] probably thinks the forest reserve should be converted to farms," Solomon hissed.

No wonder our Maasai prisoners thought this was a lark. No wonder our forest guards weren't interested in braving elephants and buffalos to catch them. How was I to overcome this obstacle? Disillusioned, I fell into a dark blue funk that lasted all the way back to Ngorongoro. My companions were no help, as the whole lot, including our former prisoners, spent the entire trip discussing the other cases they had heard that day—courtroom connoisseurs, the bunch of them. I went to bed that night with a headache. Next day I learned that the month's gas ration was finished. I was grounded again.

Grass Fires

"Go on!"

"Stop!"

"Hurry up you fool!"

"Musa, sing us a song!"

"Get off my feet stupid!"

They were so noisy I could hardly hear the truck's horn summoning stragglers to climb aboard. A drunk on the roadside slipped and sprawled helplessly in the dirt. Someone stepped over him and climbed into the truck. Two others already there jumped off again. It was like trying to herd cats.

"Where's our equipment?" I yelled at the two forest officers, who were theoretically in charge.

"What equipment?" they screamed back over the noise.

A grass fire was burning into the crater. Started by someone—Maasai herder or careless tourist—on the crater rim, it was creeping down the crater wall near Windy Gap. This was bad news. In the

1960's, foresters and park wardens didn't like fires. Many were even skeptical about controlled burns. But, that said, we had specific reasons for worrying about this fire. For one thing, it might reach and damage Munge Swamp and perhaps even Lerai Forest. It would certainly create charred grasslands that spoiled the view for tourists. And, if it moved any distance across the crater floor, it might turn and burn back up the crater wall again with disastrous consequences—fires burning upslope were especially hot and destructive. We decided that once the fire reached the crater floor where we could get at it, we would put it out.

There was still time, but at the rate our arrangements were progressing, I wondered if we were even going to get there, much less put the fire out. And I had further misgivings. Transport? A dump truck. Water? Only for drinking and that in a dented forty-four gallon drum that was already leaking. Trained fire fighters? A conscripted mob. Equipment? None, apparently. As for leadership, well….

That's not to say that I was an expert fire fighter. I had only been on one fire before, ten years earlier, while working for the Washington State Department of Forestry, and the occasion had been more amusing than instructive. When the alarm sounded, the fire crew raced out of the bunkhouse and piled hurriedly into the fire truck. With the accelerator floor-boarded, we headed down the busy interstate highway—red lights flashing and siren screaming—only to discover that someone had thoughtfully installed a governor restricting the truck's speed to well below the official speed limit. We hurried along at forty miles per hour (but making ninety mph-worth of commotion about it) while everyone else on the road whizzed by at sixty. Children waved from the back windows of passing cars. Their parents shot us amused grins. And our driver, who couldn't see the incongruity of the situation, stubbornly refused to turn off either the light or siren despite lots of yelling and pounding on the truck cab by the crew riding in the back. By the time we got there, the fire was out.

Forest officers Mlangai and Onesemo had fought fires before, so

I put them in charge. I would come along and watch. They began by getting Solomon ole Saibull to authorize the use of a truck to haul the fire fighters. Solomon also said we could use his Land Rover station wagon, which he *thought* was next door at the house of Anthony Mgina, the senior assistant conservator. But when he accompanied us there, he found no Land Rover; we would have to do without it.

It was about then that I noticed my colleagues didn't share my sense of urgency. Instead of rushing off and getting the truck and fire fighters readied, they idled about making polite small talk with some of Anthony's female relatives who had recently arrived by bus. "How was your trip? Yes, it is a dusty road isn't it? Will you be staying long?" Only then did we go to the garage to get the truck, Solomon and the forest officers recounting their experiences with wild fires along the way.

Fortunately there was a truck, a British Bedford, still in its proper place and available for use. Of course, the driver assigned to it wasn't there, as the official workday had ended hours ago. We waited while Solomon went to the junior staff quarters to ferret him out. Then we waited some more while Solomon argued with two men about something completely unrelated to the fire. Only after Solomon had, as usual, carried the day did he and Forest Officer Mlangai begin organizing the fire crew. Turning to the crowd of interested onlookers that had gathered they called out: *"Karibu lorry! Twende kupiga moto!"* Come get in the truck and let's hit the fire!

At first the crowd, composed mostly of employees of the Conservation Unit, just stood there grinning at us and talking among themselves. The more quick-witted, especially those in the back of the crowd, quickly removed themselves from the scene altogether. Finally, twenty or so men, probably realizing they had no choice because they'd been spotted and identified by their supervisors, climbed aboard. The two forest officers and I quickly followed. The truck clanked into gear and off we roared.

Despite the number of people already in the truck, the driver repeatedly stopped along the road so that the men in the back, who apparently wanted to share their fate with as many others as possible, could cajole pedestrians to join them. In this way, the crowd of fire fighters grew even larger as we progressed in fits and starts down the road.

Then we stopped again, to fill the truck's fuel tank at the local *duka*. Off everyone jumped, some to grab a quick beer, others to exhort the small groups of drinkers sitting in the sunshine to come, too. Others, having changed their minds, slipped away into the bushes. When the truck driver leaned on the horn to indicate that he was ready to go, few heeded him at first. But eventually, everyone clambered back in, although the more-inebriated ones had to be helped. Our number, however, seemed not to have increased any: we had lost as many men as we had gained.

Off we roared, this time back down the road to headquarters where—this was really getting exasperating!—the truck driver stopped to blow the horn in hopes of picking up stragglers. Two hours had passed since the fire was first noticed and we hadn't even cleared headquarters yet. Only an hour and a half remained until sunset. (I'm not a type A personality—far from it—but this was driving me nuts.)

There were no further volunteers—the headquarters compound had strangely emptied out. We continued on, only, to my complete horror, to stop yet again just before Windy Gap where we would descend into the crater. And, once again, everyone tumbled out of the truck.

"What the hell is it now?" I demanded of the two forest officers.

"Bwana, we must cut branches to beat out the fire," they replied.

"Oh!" I'd forgotten about the equipment.

So we lopped branches from leafy shrubs and stacked them in the back of the truck; other than using our feet to stamp out the flames, they were to be the only equipment we had. This was my introduction to what the rural development profession calls "appropriate technology."

Twenty minutes later we were ready to go again when two of the men, misinformed as to just where we were to hit the fire, trotted off to where it still burned along the top of the crater rim. After a lot of arm-waving and screaming by the others, they eventually returned and we set off again.

Shortly after we started down the Windy Gap track into the crater, we squeezed a Land Rover full of tourists high up on the inside bank of the steep, narrow road. The track was officially one-way down, but tour drivers often came up it anyway because it was the fastest route to the lodge. The tourists were furious but we didn't care because, just then, the fire came into view and the men, who were becoming increasingly excited, suddenly exploded into song. They sang in the Mbulu language, so I couldn't understand them, but that didn't matter because the sound was so moving that the words would probably have spoiled it for me. The truck bumped and skidded, its cargo of sweaty bodies swaying and lurching as they chanted in two-part harmony, led by a husky voice in front. Some of the lyrics must have been hilarious, judging by how often the singers broke off to collapse in laughter.

Bouncing over the grass to the fire which, despite all my worrying, was only just now reaching the crater floor, the truck stopped and our crew jumped out, grabbed their branches and, with excited shouts, went on the attack. Despite everyone doing it his own way while loudly giving advice to his neighbors, the men whaled away at the flames with such vigor that they soon extinguished the part of the fire burning on the crater floor. Then they turned their attention to extinguishing what they could of the part that was still burning on the lower crater wall.

Here, in some of the gullies, there were occasional patches of tall grass that were just too hot to put out by whacking with our now heavily singed shrub branches. Instead, the two forest officers set backfires—now that some technical expertise was called for, these gentlemen suddenly came into their own. They backfired up one gully and then the next, the men following behind beating out a firebreak as the wind pushed the fire into the oncoming blaze. Soon that fire was out too, although we stayed until 9 p.m. to make sure. High above us near the rim, more flames were slowly eating their way down the crater wall; we might be able to extinguish those tomorrow by coming in over the top. Several miles across the crater to the northeast, a thin glowing tracery of red spreading slowly down the crater wall marked another fire to which we would have to attend. Not tonight, however.

During the next dry season, a fire came to life on the high grassy plateau northeast of the crater. Plumes of smoke were common features of the dry-season landscape when fires occurred for a variety of reasons. Set to smoke bees or to clear dry grass for next season's grazing, they usually soon went out again. This one didn't.

The previous rainy season had produced so much grass—more than the resident herbivores could consume—that fuel was abundant. The fire bypassed some spots because they were yet too green to burn, others because they had been heavily grazed. Leisurely, it made its ragged way down the wall onto the crater floor. At night the fire showed as a sometimes-wavy, often-broken, brightly glowing, thread, a shaky calligraphic scrawl across a black velvet wall hanging. Unlike a wall hanging, however, the pattern changed every night.

Each morning the fire re-awakened after a still, cool night. Confining itself at first to slow starts and cautious exploration, it became more active as the temperature and wind increased. On hot, windy afternoons, when it was wide awake, it whooshed and crackled across the crater floor. Swallows and rollers swooped through the smoke feeding on insects disturbed by the flames and gangly secretary birds stalked along its front, picking off fleeing snakes and lizards. As the fire progressed, it left behind a blanket of grayish black ash stirred here and there by the wind into spiraling "ash devils."

Eventually, the fire reached the Munge River. Unable to cross, it moved along the stream's southern bank deeper into the center of the crater, parts of the fire surging greedily through the dry grass while pushing up vast amounts of smoke, other parts hesitating, fizzling, smoldering, almost dying out. However, slowly here, quickly there, progress it did until it came to the Munge (Mandusi) Swamp, which it entered and slowly but inexorably began to reduce to ashes.

Munge Swamp was small, only two to three square miles in area, but its dense stands of tall sedges were unique within the Conservation Area. Consequently, the conservator felt a strong obligation to preserve the swamp. He instructed me to put the fire out.

Two truckloads of laborers hit the fire that afternoon. The fire had slowed after entering the swamp, so there was still something left to save. Spilling out of the trucks, the men enthusiastically attacked the fire with gunny sacks and branches cut from shrubs on the crater rim, whomping the ground at the base of the flames to remove the oxygen and, thereby, also the flames. Unfortunately, while this technique worked on small, tired, unenthusiastic fires, it was less effective against an ambitious one like this. The flames emitted a startled *whoosh* when struck, but immediately resumed burning again. Poor organization—the men flailing away wherever and whenever they felt like it—exacerbated the situation.

I divided them into teams of several men each, and instructed each team to line up next to the fire and then, in unison, give a great wop at its base with their branches. Then they were to step ahead and, all together, hit it again. That way each foot of ground along the fire's leading edge would get whacked several times over as the team passed by— *whoomp* (step), *whoomp* (step), *whoomp* (step). I gave a quick demonstration, then stepped back and let them go to it. Grunting in unison as they struck—ughh-*whoomp* (step), ughh-*whoomp* (step), ughh-*whoomp* (step)—they immediately began to have an effect. A single pass of beaters along a section of the fire's front was sufficient to check its advance. The tempo increased when men dropped aside to chant and keep the rhythm going. They praised their own team, insulted the others, made fun of the young *mzungu* (as I later discovered), and described the amount of beer they would later drink. The fire was out by nightfall. Tired but jubilant, the men retired to the trucks, drank with great gulps from rubber hoses leading from forty-four gallon drums of water, rested, then mounted the trucks and rode home, singing and stamping. I was tired but content.

However, setting off the next morning to walk to the office where I would modestly accept the conservator's "Well done sir!" my buoyant feelings of well-being suddenly evaporated. The Munge Swamp was burning again. So, off we all went: trucks, laborers, and I, back into the crater to fight the Munge Swamp fire again, and again we put it right out. This time, we waited an additional hour to make sure it was well and truly dead before going home. There was no singing and stamping on the way home.

The swamp was burning again the next morning. And it burned on several mornings after that until the fire, having destroyed everything in the swamp, went out of its own accord. By then I knew why I had failed to extinguish it. Over the years, the natural mortality of sedges in the swamp had built up a layer of dead plants several feet deep. It was this that was slowly burning, and not just at the surface where we could see it, but right down through all that dead material to ground (or sometimes water) level. Even when the fire seemed to be out, it was still smoldering away, out of sight. Every morning it found its way to the surface again and erupted into flame.

For awhile, my self-image suffered. Retiring from the public's eye, I made skillful use of the bushes between house and office to avoid meetings with amused colleagues. I skipped office tea breaks, and took long safaris into the bush at the slightest excuse. Eventually, however, life returned to normal.

The dry season ended and the rains came, the grass grew again and the color of the crater floor changed from the buff of dry grass to light green. The exceptions were areas burnt completely bare last dry season. Within days of the first rain, they changed from ashy-black to brilliant, emerald green, there being no dry grass to dilute the color. Grazers—Thomson's and Grant's gazelle, wildebeest, zebra, kongoni—promptly moved onto the old burn, attracted by young succulent grass.

But the greatest change was in Munge Swamp. In the past, the swamp had looked much the same throughout the year. Wildlife hadn't used it much. Now dense stands of dark green aeschynomene (a type of vetch) suddenly shot up, some of them twelve feet high. Small or medium-sized grazers avoided the dense vegetation, possibly because predators could hide there; but larger animals made frequent visits. Rhinos especially loved this sweet leguminous shrub, and used the swamp more than ever before.

And it was all because of the fire that refused to go out. Over the years, dead stems and leaf litter had accumulated on the floor of the swamp. Seeds had to struggle through the choking mass to germinate. Released from this suffocating blanket, the swamp was revitalized. The Conservation Unit had wanted to save Munge Swamp. It just hadn't occurred to anyone that the best way to do so was to let it burn.

The conservator, impressed by the results of the Munge Swamp fire, decided to put the lesson to practical use in the northwestern part of the crater. Like Munge Swamp before it was burned, this area also was little-used by wildlife. So much dead, unpalatable plant material had built up that grazing animals simply were not attracted to the area any more. If we were to burn it, the next rains would green it up with tender new grass which would attract wildebeest, zebra, and other grazing animals. The entire area needed burning but we decided to test our methods first with a small experimental burn.

We selected the top of Engitati Hill for the experiment. Engitati, which rises near the northwestern edge of Munge Swamp, is a small, collapsed volcano with a slightly concave top—a volcano within Ngorongoro's volcano. The top of the hill seemed a perfect site for an experimental burn because it was largely ungrazed (offering plenty of fuel) and fully encircled by a game-viewing track which would act as a firebreak.

One sunny morning John Goddard and I, together with a truckload of laborers, arrived at the hilltop. First we set a backfire to keep the fire from jumping the firebreak, and posted thirty or so laborers downwind to extinguish sparks blown outside the burn area. We didn't expect many sparks because the wind was mild, the morning cool, and the proposed burn area small. Then we began torching the dry grass inside the bowl.

Everything went as planned. John and I watched the fire flame and smoke its way across the hilltop, meet the backfire, and sputter out leaving only a few scattered patches of grass still smoldering within the controlled burn area. The waiting laborers promptly dispatched the few sparks that blew across the firebreak. After standing around for a while doing nothing, we decided to go home, leaving the men to hang around another hour or two on the remote chance that another spark blew over the firebreak. Now, it was simply a matter of waiting until the next rains. We would return then to count the animals attracted to the fresh green grass.

We even stopped at the lodge to have a self-congratulatory drink. Hubris. We should have known better.

When we walked in, the lodge's picture windows were three deep in voluble tourists. Others were running back to their rooms to get binoculars and cameras. The attraction was a huge fire about eight miles away, which, I recognized with sinking heart, had originated at Engitati hill. It had already burned across two miles of grassland and was now swiftly crackling its way up the crater wall to the forest on the rim. Individual trees and large bushes could be seen exploding into flame ("Oo's" and "Ah's" from the tourists) as the fire rushed up the steep slope, its dense smoke completely obscuring Olmoti, the flat-topped mountain north of the crater. The lodge hummed with excitement; the onlookers were getting something more than their tour brochures had promised.

"I say!" A Brit expostulated. "Does this happen every year?"

There were no drinks at the lodge for us that day. We quietly eased back out the door and slunk home, our professional tails between our legs. What an unmitigated disaster! We were responsible for one of the biggest burns on the crater floor in years, and one that had actually gotten into the prized forest atop the crater rim. What in Heaven's name had happened?

What had happened, as we later learned, was that soon after John and I left, a gust of wind blew sparks down the side of the hill where they caught and began to burn in the dry grass. Several men ran with gunny sacks to extinguish the small fires. And they surely would have succeeded, had they not been chased away by a heretofore unnoticed rhino. Everyone piled into the truck. Trying to frighten the rhino away, the driver ran the truck at it, honked the horn and revved the engine. Everybody yelled. The rhino stood firm. Soon the grass near the rhino began smoking, the wind picked up, and the rest is history.

I don't know whether animals ever did come in greater numbers to the burned area after the next rains. I suppose we must have counted them, but I don't remember. I don't even remember what Solomon, the conservator, had to say to us about it. The trauma of losing control of our "controlled" burn, and letting fire get into forest on the crater rim overpowers all other memories of the occasion. However, I do remember that it was the only time I ever heard John Goddard say, "Damn that rhino!"

Plains, Craters, and People

Welcoming Herman to Africa

Hissing steam suddenly geysered from under the hood of the car. Damn! We were in trouble. And it was my fault, too, because I hadn't checked the water in the radiator when we rented the car earlier that day in Arusha. The Indian proprietor said the car was "Very ready to go please!" and I just took his word for it.

Now here I was, deep in the bush with a nonfunctioning vehicle full of people and no spare water. Walking the several miles it would take to get help was not a happy prospect. There were buffaloes about; we'd passed a herd of them a few minutes earlier. Elephants were nearby; we could see fresh piles of their dung on the road. No, I was definitely not interested in walking. Furthermore, we seemed to be the only people around. There hadn't been another vehicle on the road for some time. Frustrated, I looked at Herman. Exasperated, Herman stared back at me. The two passengers in the back seat, Jo and Judy, Peace Corps nurses from Arusha, glared accusingly at both of us. It was an awkward situation. Something had to be done. But I had no idea what. Turning again to my colleague in the front seat, I gestured helplessly and exclaimed, "Welcome to Africa, Herman."

It had all started the day before when, after spending a difficult day helping Herman, a new NCA staff member, extract a needed household item from the Public Works Department (PWD) storehouse, I took him with me to visit Jo and Judy in their small house on the hospital grounds. I wanted to say goodbye because they were packing up to leave for the USA. We found them at home, slouched in their government-issue PWD arm chairs and looking hot and harassed, fed up with the tedious rigor of packing, and ready to be distracted. They quickly produced both tea and conversation. At first it was stupid PWD this, and frigging packing that, but eventually other topics began to emerge, in particular the fact that Jo and Judy had lived in Arusha for two years now and still hadn't photographed a number of sights that actually defined the place. Neither had they visited the small but very popular Ngurdoto Crater National Park, which lay only about twenty miles away, just east of Mt. Meru. As it turned out, neither had I.

"What a shame we never got photos," said Jo, sadly.

"I've only some of this house," said Judy.

"What will I show my grandchildren?" lamented Jo, who was a matronly fifty-something.

"My family will think Africa's a little wooden house with an avocado tree in front," moaned Judy.

"If I wasn't essentially broke," continued Jo, "I'd rent a car and go take all those pictures and see those places."

"Yeah, same here!" agreed Judy.

"And it's actually quite cheap, too," said Jo, doggedly maintaining the car-rental theme. "I wish we knew someone who could afford to rent a car for a few days."

"Somebody who would do it as a parting gift to two good friends whom he may never see again," added Judy.

At this point, both women, probably checking if I wanted more tea, turned and gazed directly at me.

I commiserated with them while Judy refilled my cup with fresh tea and Jo pushed a plate of cookies under my nose. Yes, indeed, they had my sympathy. I understood about inadequate volunteer salaries. ("No thank you Jo, I don't need another cushion; I'm quite comfortable.") I recognized that flaw in human nature that makes us put things off to the very last until it's too late to remedy the situation ("Yes, thanks Judy, I will have some more sugar."), where one is left, surrounded by half-full packing boxes ("Another cookie? You bet."), and feeling sad because there's no one around to assist with a bit of spare cash to—then it hit me: *I* could rent a car! Jo and Judy were so overcome by this unexpected suggestion that, for the first time in several minutes, they broke eye contact—up to now they'd been hanging on my every word—and stopped plying me with tea and cookies. Relaxing back into their armchairs, they broke into contented smiles.

"Why Dennis," they murmured, "how nice. Why didn't we think of that?"

Unfortunately, the smiles faded when I remembered I also was short on funds. Having recently handed out several "loans" to junior staff at Ngorongoro, I was presently little better off than the nurses. The gloom cast by this discovery was beginning to thicken when, with a single mind, the nurses focused on Herman. They didn't speak but their thoughts were clear: Herman was not a volunteer so he probably had some money; he was my colleague and, therefore, by association, also theirs; he had drunk their tea and eaten their cookies … Poor Herman. Up to now only on the edge of the conversation, he was suddenly the center of attention as three sets of eyes regarded him with hungry anticipation.

Consequently, Herman rented a car from the United Touring Co., and we drove around town while the nurses took their photographs: the old German *boma;* colorful jacaranda, Nandi flame, and flamboyant trees; the clock tower in the traffic circle; Wameru huts half-hidden by banana trees. Next morning we drove to Ngurdoto Crater National Park. We found the Crater to be a pleasant little place, with forest spilling down its shallow inner walls and a floor carpeted with grass. We saw a rhino, twelve giraffe, a large herd of buffalo, and many wart hogs. The nurses were pleased. From there we drove a few miles through dense forest and bush to Momela Lakes. Water birds were abundant, especially large white pelicans squatting in groups by the water or flying overhead in long, slowly undulating strings. And that's when it happened. Herman and I were busy identifying birds when the nurses, whose attention had wandered, asked us why steam was issuing from under the car's hood.

Fortunately we found an empty Coke bottle beneath one of the seats—luckily the rental agency hadn't cleaned the car recently. We waited until the radiator cooled down, took the bottle to the lake to fill (adding our footprints in the mud to those of buffalo, elephant, rhino, and various types of buck), returned to the car, and poured the slimy green water into the radiator. Once the radiator was full—it took a lot of trips—we heaved a sigh of relief, scraped the mud off our feet, piled back into the car, and returned to Arusha.

That evening I jokingly suggested to Herman that today's lesson was to always take a Coke bottle on safari. He didn't laugh. A recent arrival to Africa, Herman was contending with a cultural environment considerably more laid back (and less efficient) than he was used to. He'd been piling up painful learning experiences right and left, and didn't appreciate my landing him in yet another. In my opinion, he was adjusting—he'd threatened to quit and return to Canada only twice in the past three days—but he wasn't doing it easily.

A senior-level research scientist with the Canadian Wildlife Service, Herman Dirschl was at Ngorongoro under the auspices of the Canadian International Development Aid Program to prepare a management and development plan for the Conservation Area. He had first to learn everything he could about the Conservation Area—climate, geology, soils, vegetation, wildlife, people, land uses—and the structure, policies, and activities of the Conservation Unit. Then he would use this information to propose ways in which the conservator and his staff could better develop and manage the Ngorongoro Conservation Area. He had one year.

Herman moved his family, consisting of his attractive wife Maria and their baby son, into an empty senior staff house on the lip of the crater, and got down to business. Soon he was a familiar sight, striding purposefully about the compound arranging meetings (we became used to Herman's hailing us with upraised hand and wide smile: "Ah, good. Can we talk?"), collecting and reading reports, and scribbling away at his desk. This was BC—Before Computers—and the Conservation Unit's few typewriters were confined to the conservator's office.

Herman's ready smile disguised a serious disposition. He had high professional standards and could become irritated when others didn't live up to them, which frequently happened. His approach to life was reflected in the way he kept his desk. It was clean and ordered. There was no clutter of dog-eared files and loose papers; no large maps kept from rolling back into themselves by the judicious placement of a mug of yesterday's tea; no stubby, chewed-up pencils with missing erasers lost in the litter of unread reports, T-squares, and aerial photographs. I mean, Herman kept nothing on his desk but a few pencils (with erasers) and a clean pad of paper aligned precisely with the desk's edge. To give him the benefit of the doubt, he was too new yet to have gotten his desk properly seasoned. However, you couldn't get around that severe geometrical alignment of paper and pencils with its implied expectation of an orderly universe. As I had found this to be notable in Tanganyika chiefly by its absence, I deduced that Herman was in for some serious culture shock.

And I was correct. One week after his arrival, Herman's introduction to the cultural and logistical realities of Africa was well underway. The vehicle promised to him in his contract didn't exist. He was rapidly learning that "Right away sir" often meant sometime next week (maybe), and that the answer "Yes" didn't necessarily indicate agreement or that the speaker even understood the question. That there were funds allocated for his work in the Conservation Unit's budget didn't mean that he could actually spend them. Or if he could, it was only after excruciatingly long delays while the proper bureaucratic procedures were followed; or not in the amounts needed because of unexpected cuts imposed by the Ministry. Private businesses frequently wouldn't accept Government Local Purchase Orders because the Ministry was so slow to reimburse them. Materials and equipment were scarce or nonexistent or a hundred miles distant in Arusha. Camping equipment allocated to him in the central storeroom was being used by someone else. People hanging about the Conservation Unit's compound bugged him by peering in through the windows of his office. Several had already asked him for "loans." Herman's temper first became noticeable during this period.

Nevertheless, Herman soon made his presence felt, not least in helping me persuade the conservator that I should do less road building and more research. Within a month of his arrival, I was doing something I'd wanted to do for some time: prepare a map of the vegetation communities of the Ngorongoro Conservation Area. The map would contribute to an inventory of biotic diversity, and help identify wildlife and livestock habitats.

Herman often came along on these safaris, partly to help, but also to experience at first hand the varied landscapes of the Conservation Area. He wanted to actually see what he was writing about in his management and development plan. Walking and driving cross-country, guided by aerial photos that showed us the terrain and gross features of the vegetation, we recorded the presence and abundance of plant species—grasses, sedges, forbs, shrubs, trees—on plots and along transects. With every safari our knowledge of plant names progressed, and we were able to identify more plant communities. Each was interesting in it's own way, for instance, *Pennisetum clandestinum* (Kikuyu grass) grassland, which is smooth and green (and almost as low) as the baize on a billiard table; or *Themeda triandra* (red oat grass) grassland, which seemed to burn a lot and, when dry, tinted the landscape a distinctive reddish brown; or Commiphora woodland, which is dominated by a close relative of the tree that produces myrrh (as in frankincense and myrrh); and so on. Mapping vegetation was fascinating work. I loved it.

From a high summit we watched small ephemeral storms daub the Serengeti Plains with pools of glittering water. We drove through acres of grassland colored by fragrant yellow, purple, and violet flowers. We listened to small green and orange Fischer's love birds twitter and whistle as they drank from pools of water. At Kakesio, a small village thirty miles southwest of Ngorongoro, we rested beneath a pink-flowered Cape chestnut tree savoring the view over huts and cornfields to the hills and mountains beyond Lake Eyasi.

At the government rest house at Endulen, an agricultural settlement halfway between Kakesio and Ngorongoro, we encountered special khaki-clad police searching for cattle thieves. A giant sergeant, who could easily have torn a telephone book in half, welcomed us with a genial smile, vacated half of the building for our use, and invited us to dinner—*ugali* with meat relish. Next morning he and his men packed up and drove away in a convoy of Land Rovers. As each vehicle passed by—Herman and I were standing by the road at the time—the men inside grinned and waved and honked their horns, leading Herman to quip, "I feel like I'm reviewing the troops." Then, just as the last vehicle disappeared around a corner, there came the loud—and because it was so unexpected—hair-raising wail of a siren. The police had sirens! It was startling—eerie, even—to hear them in such an isolated place. We couldn't imagine their purpose, except perhaps to wow the inhabitants of small bush villages.

It was on these safaris that I noticed another thing about Herman. Whereas I typically came back looking and smelling like I'd slept in my shirt and pants and never washed (often the case, actually), Herman always seemed to have just stepped from a clothing store after visiting a barber. I don't know how he did it; he just had this *flair*.

That Christmas, Herman and Maria invited me for dinner. While taped Christmas music filled the room, they plied me with roast yearling wildebeest, two kinds of wine, brandy, cake, candies, and cookies. Then they gave me a very nice meerschaum pipe as a present. As I returned to my little house that night, I realized that the Dirschls wouldn't be here next Christmas. I was going to miss them.

A grass fire burns on the floor of Ngorongoro Crater. The dark-colored vegetation is Gorgor Swamp. Lolmalasin Mountain rises beyond the crater.

Dennis Herlocker

The author (left) and Herman Dirschl, at the Endulen government rest house twelve miles southwest of Ngorongoro. (Photo courtesy of Herman Dirschl.)

Some Crater Happenings

My association with John Goddard involved me with other biologists, one of whom, an American by the name of Dick Estes, was studying the behavior and ecology of Ngorongoro Crater's wildebeest population.

A wildebeest is a brindled, dull slate gray beast with a foolish expression, incongruous body parts (large front, small rear, spindly legs), and a gait like a rocking horse. *A Field Guide to the Larger Mammals of Africa* describes it as "the old fool of the veldt."

On the other hand, the wildebeest is ecologically important. In the 1960's it was the most abundant game species in Ngorongoro Crater: over half of all large mammals in the crater were wildebeest. Consequently, wildebeests were the principal food for large predators, and the primary grazers of the crater's grassland vegetation. Removing wildebeest from the crater would be a disaster for lions and hyenas. Uneaten grass on the crater floor would grow rank and sour. Dead grass would accumulate, excluding smaller grazers, such as Thomson's gazelle, which prefer a short grass habitat, and resulting in destructive wildfires which would sweep across the crater floor and up the walls into the forest. The result would be fewer species, fewer animals, and a much less-interesting place to visit. Dick Estes had good reason to study wildebeest.

Dick had to use somewhat different methods to study wildebeest than John Goddard used for his rhino. There were over 25,000 of them and they all looked alike, yet somehow Dick had to be able to find and observe selected animals. He did this by marking them so that they could be easily spotted again and identified. The problem, of course, was how to make them stand still long enough to be marked.

Until the early 1960's, large mammals such as wildebeest and rhino were captured by roping them from a chase vehicle, a technique demonstrated in the movie *Hatari* (Danger), filmed in the crater and its surroundings in the late 1950's. In *Hatari*, John Wayne and his crew of professional big game catchers pursued rhinos with Land Rovers, and caught them with a lasso held at the end of a long stick. Unfortunately, stressing animals in this way often killed them, as was rumored to have happened to several rhinos during the filming of *Hatari*.

By the mid 1960's, however, scientists and capture teams were immobilizing animals with a hollow drug-filled dart fired from a special type of air rifle. An animal was chosen from the herd, its weight estimated by eye, the amount of drug thought to be proper for that species and weight placed in the hollow dart, and the dart loaded into the air rifle. Then the shooter eased within firing range and plunked the dart into the animal's backside. After a few minutes the animal grew woozy, staggered about for a while, and finally fell down.

At least it usually happened that way. John and I were lending Dick Estes a hand once when the dart hit the animal but failed to inject the drug. The startled wildebeest pounded away forcing the darting crew to chase after it to get the dart back (they were expensive). Across the bumpy crater floor we sped. Just as we were drawing within range again, and the rifleman was leaning out the window drawing a bead on his moving, twisting target, we hit a hyena hole. Whump! Heads dented the cab roof and people standing in the back landed in a heap on the pickup's bed. We had to stop to get everyone sorted out as the wildebeest drummed away.

Once a darted animal was down, cars roared up and disgorged people who, depending on the animal species and purpose of immobilization (Dick wasn't the only scientist to dart animals in the crater), quickly began taking measurements, fixing marking and/or tracking devices, taking blood samples, and collecting ticks. If needed, others poured water on the animal to cool it down, or cushioned it against harm from involuntary muscle spasms. I once found myself stuffing gunny sacks of grass beneath the head of an immobilized rhino that, unable to move in any other way, was endangering itself by repeatedly banging its head sideways against the ground. Richard Leaky, who had driven up from Oldupai Gorge for the occasion, quickly joined me, and together we sat on the rhino's head to keep it still. Speed was of the essence because animals varied widely in their response to the drug. Occasionally, an average dose would kill an animal or, alternatively, it might wear off sooner than expected.

The expatriate staff and African students of a wildlife management institute learned this the hard way while practicing immobilization techniques in the crater. They wanted to immobilize a rhino as an exercise, so they chose Horace, the most docile rhino in the crater. At first everything went as planned: the convoy of trucks and Land Rovers descended into the crater, found Horace, drove up beside the unsuspecting animal, and shot him in the rear with a dart. With a startled "Huff!," Horace whirled to face his adversary, but the drug quickly took effect and he was soon stretched on his side, with students swarming over him wielding measuring tapes, clipboards, syringes, and specimen bottles.

Marking a captured wildebeest in Ngorongoro Crater: Penny Goddard (in Land Rover), the author (holding the tail), John Goddard, and a British volunteer (who seems to be doing most of the work).

It was about noon. Now that the entertainment was over (or so they thought), and Horace had another hour or so to sleep off the drug, the staff wives spread white tablecloths on the grass near the recumbent rhino and loaded them with tableware, thermoses of tea, and plates of sandwiches and cakes. Then everyone—staff, students, wives and children (visiting on holiday from boarding schools in England)—reposed themselves for lunch.

Suddenly Horace lurched to his feet. The effects of the drug had worn off prematurely. Women screamed, kids yelled, and men swore as the befuddled rhino bumped into cars and charged towards or fled from sudden movements (of which there were naturally a great many). Everyone ran for the cars where they either got inside as fast as possible or hid behind them, while Horace careened about, denting cars and breaking windows, squashing cakes and food hampers, overturning sample jars, and goring and dragging through the dirt beautifully starched and ironed white linen tablecloths imported from England. He was still trailing one from his horn as he weaved away across the crater floor.

Dick Estes eventually stopped darting wildebeest because the drugs were too unreliable.

To expedite his fieldwork, Dick constructed a cabin, twelve by eighteen, under a large fig tree at the edge of the Munge River. He often let others use the cabin when he wasn't there. We called it Munge (or Estes) Camp.

I once had an exciting night at Munge Camp, together with a number of other Conservation Unit people including Philip ole Seyalel, his driver, and several laborers. Herman Dirschl, the Ngorongoro Conservation Unit's ecologist, had sent them to fence a small plot of grassland near the center of the crater. The idea was to keep animals from eating the grass that grew inside the fence. Herman would then measure grass production and use that to estimate how much forage was available to grazers on the crater floor.

There were many tents (the cabin could only sleep a few people) and Land Rovers, so it was quite an encampment. The two senior officers, Philip ole Seyalel and I, pulled rank on the others, claimed the cabin and flipped a coin for the only bed. Philip lost, so he had to sleep on the floor.

We both slept soundly until about two in the morning when, suddenly, from outside, there came a terrified scream, followed by shouting, more screaming, the sounds of people running about, yelled questions, and car doors slamming. Engines started up and raced wildly. Horns blared. Jumping out of bed, I ran to the door, stumbling over Philip on the way. Outside, inadequately clothed people rushed about tripping over tent ropes, banging on car doors, shouting at one another. Someone was repeatedly flashing a Land Rover's headlights on and off. Another car, its horn blaring, was being driven fast around and around in a tight circle at the edge of camp. Quickly surveying the tents, I found all erect except for one that was drooping badly and seemed to have developed a second door.

Eventually, the racket abated and I was able to inquire into what had happened, although it took some time to get a coherent picture. Apparently a lion, probably young, had walked through the camp and noticed a tent's loose window flap waving in the light breeze. Playfully, the lion began batting it. Inside the tent, someone woke to see the silhouette of a lion pawing at the canvas just above his head, and roused the camp with a piercing scream. Startled, the lion instinctively reacted by taking a real swipe at the tent this time, rending it from top to bottom, which brought louder shouts and screams from inside. Then, probably frightened by all the noise, the lion ran away. As for the man squirreling about in the Land Rover at the edge of camp, he claimed he had chased away an entire pride of lions. Possibly he had.

Most everyone spent the rest of the night in the Land Rovers.

A few months later, Philip and I were helping Herman measure grass production within his small fenced plot. We worked late that day clipping samples of grass. By the time we filled the last gunny sack with cut grass, all tourists had long since left the game-viewing tracks on the crater floor and returned to the lodge on the crater rim. Except for a single Maasai *boma* a few miles away, and a large number of animals, we were in sole possession of the crater. We loaded our sacks of grass into the Land Rover and drove over to Munge Camp where we planned to eat some beans, remove the sharp-pointed grass seeds that had lodged in our socks during the day, and get some sleep. However, if we had looked forward to doing this in privacy, we were to be disappointed.

We arrived at the cabin to find a large group of Maasai *murran* in full warrior kit including spears, short swords, clubs, and even a few large buffalo-hide shields. Some were slaughtering a cow. Others were preparing a fire over which the cow was to be roasted. A number were dancing, leaping pogo stick-like into the air, ramrod straight with spears held vertically at their sides: "G*runt*," (into the air), slap (sandals hit the ground), "G*runt*," slap, "G*runt*," slap, on and on, until the first two warriors quit and another two replaced them.

It was soon clear that we were not welcome. Hard-faced *murran* belligerently surrounded our Land Rover, shouting questions at Philip, a Maasai himself, about why we were here and what our intentions were. Only grudgingly did they let us out of the car and into the cabin.

Once inside, Philip explained. Just as we had not expected to see them, neither had the *murran* expected us. They were on their way to punish the Wasukuma, who had had the temerity, several days previously, to raid a Maasai *boma* southwest of the crater and make off with its livestock. Since intertribal conflicts of any sort were strictly outlawed by the government, which would have intervened in the squabble with truckloads of heavily armed police, the *murran* had planned to pass through the crater at night when nobody was around who might tip off the authorities. Now, suddenly, here we were—government officials— just the people likely to interfere.

They were mollified when Philip explained that we were not returning to headquarters for another two days and had no radio with which to contact the police. Nonetheless, they made it clear that we were under house arrest until they left sometime during the night.

We were safe enough: at the worst, they might puncture our Land Rover's tires with their spears. Still....

The Maasai tribe was widely known for its bellicosity, its warriors for their fearlessness and savagery. For at least two hundred years, Maasai herdsmen had lorded over thousands of square miles of East Africa. From their homeland in the extensive grassy plains of present-day southern Kenya and northern Tanzania, they had raided far and wide, keeping neighboring peoples in constant fear. Even well-armed Arab ivory and slave-trading caravans from the coast were bullied and taxed (plundered might be a better word for it) if they passed through Maasai territory.

Nowadays, of course, the Maasai were less feared—the government had all of the guns—although they were still greatly respected for their martial abilities. Nevertheless, the men feasting and dancing outside our cabin that night were trained and disciplined warriors eagerly looking forward to a good fight. I felt sorry for the Wasukuma.

That evening we were sitting in the small hut, subdued somewhat by the rowdy bunch swaggering about outside loudly proclaiming what they would do to the Wasukuma (Philip said it involved breaking heads and poking holes in people), when we heard a voice at the door, "*Hodi?*"

Opening up, we found a *murrani* regarding us with level gaze. Unlike others in his warrior cohort, whose stocky, muscular bodies betrayed Bantu blood, he was tall and slender, a classic Maasai. Like the others, his rusty-colored, knee-length *shuka* was knotted over one shoulder, and from his pierced, elongated ear lobes dangled heavy, cone-shaped earrings. Loops of thin wire, strung with small beads, depended from the tops of his ears. His carefully plaited hair, tinted red by ocher, hung below his shoulders, while over his forehead the plaits had been drawn together to terminate in a single large knot which dangled between his eyes. A brightly beaded band of leather encircled his neck. Another adorned an arm.

He did not look effeminate. He looked tough. Arrogant. Mean. He also looked like someone who had a bone to pick and, furthermore, wanted to pick it with us. Politely, we said, "*Karibu,*" and invited him in.

Chunk! He jabbed the iron base of his spear into the soil by the door. Stepping inside, he raked the room with haughty eyes, giving us to understand that if he ever caught us stealing Maasai cattle or befriending Wasukuma, he would know what to do about it. Planting himself firmly in the center of the room, he stood for a few moments glaring disdainfully at us—like an army sergeant confronting unsatisfactory-looking recruits—before he spoke (as Philip translated):

"My name is Letema. I have killed three lions. My shield bears the marks of their claws."

Here he paused briefly to regard us with what appeared to be amused contempt—probably trying to imagine wimpy beings like us killing anything with a spear and buffalo hide shield—before he resumed speech.

"We are the *Tobola*." Then he waited for the awe to show on our faces: *Tobola* was the name given to the current age-set of Maasai warriors.

"The *Washenzi* [the uncivilized, the barbaric, in other words the non-Maasai] fear us. They flee before us! We take their cattle! We sport with their women! Even the *wazungu*, with their guns and *ndege* [airplanes—literally, birds], respect us." He fixed Herman and me with a cool, menacing stare.

At this point the short sword and wooden club stuck in his belt suddenly came into focus. Not being entirely sure where he was headed with all this, I cautiously looked around for a defensive weapon. There was nothing. Maybe I could heave a gunny sack of grass at him and escape out the door while he was distracted—Herman would have to look out for himself. The *murrani* spoke again:

"Tomorrow we raid the Wasukuma who must then deal with real *murran* rather than little herd boys. It will be good," he predicted with a grim smile.

Now a dreamy expression crossed his face as (I assumed) he contemplated walloping Wasukuma, dragging their women into the bushes, and making off with their cattle. But then he became stern again and once more fixed us with glinty, obsidian eyes. Nervously, we shifted in our seats.

"My stomach hurts."

His stomach hurts?

He stared at us for a few moments with unblinking eyes; we were too flabbergasted by this admission of weakness to respond. Then, apparently unable to contain himself any longer, he burst into a flood of speech:

"Meat upsets my stomach, which is very sensitive. Always when we go to fight, we must eat meat. It is the custom. And always I go into battle with a stomach ache. Therefore, I ask for some coffee, which I know w*azungu* drink (I drank some once and found it settled my stomach). Then I can enjoy raiding the Wasukuma, just like my brothers."

We'd been drinking coffee when he came in the door, so his request was easy to grant. So, for a time the fierce *murrani* sat with us, chatting companionably with Philip in *Maa,* their tribal language, while appreciatively drinking his coffee (with lots of milk and sugar). Finally, having determined just how he and Philip were related, and whether Philip or the *murrani's* father had the larger herd of cattle (*murran* weren't allowed to have cattle or to marry; their job was to fight), the warrior decided that his stomach was better and politely took his leave. The smell of smoke, grease, and dried sweat that he had brought in with him remained behind.

For a few minutes we sat, bemused at what we had done. By making this guy feel better (which was good), we had probably stored up trouble for several Wasukuma tomorrow (which was bad). However, instead of worrying about it, we went to bed. With the carousing that was going on outside, we would need all the sleep we could get.

Letters from Cathy

It had been another frustrating day constructing a track around the west rim of the crater. Started months ago, the work was progressing at the proverbial snail's pace because the Caterpillar bulldozer frequently broke down, and each time it did, weeks passed before it was repaired. Today had run true to form, starting with the late arrival of the Land Rover driver. Then the radiator needed filling—as did the gas tank. The clerk took his time preparing the Local Purchase Order to buy gas at Muhinda's privately owned pump. We waited again for some other NCA Land Rovers and trucks to appear (regulations required all vehicles be refueled at the same time). Then our Land Rover wouldn't start, so we had to push it. Finally, after picking up several laborers, and drums of fuel and water for the Caterpillar (pre-loading wasn't possible, because someone else had used the Land Rover the day before), we set out only to have Solomon flag us down at the gate and tell us to take some bags of cement three miles down the road in the opposite direction.

We arrived at the road head to find the tractor idle. Its driver hadn't started it yet. He wisely preferred not to disturb an elephant, a few hundred feet away that had emerged from the forest to browse. Only when the big animal left a half hour later did we begin work. Then, after clearing bush for a short distance, the bulldozer encountered a nest of bees. I re-routed the track (it doesn't pay to mess with African bees any more than elephants), but a few minutes later a large tree fell on the tractor, just missing the driver. After that the bulldozer, which had worked exactly three days since its last breakdown, wouldn't start again, and I knew from experience that whatever had broken would take at least another week to repair. I returned to Ngorongoro a grumpy volunteer: was I never going to finish this blasted track?

However, the next day I was gloomy only as long as it took to pick up my mail, which consisted of a single light blue aerogram with a brightly colored Tanganyika stamp. It was from Cathy. Quickly I ripped open the aerogram and read it. *Dear Dennis …* Then I read it again. Only then did it suddenly strike me that the sun was shining, flowers were blooming (very beautifully too, I might add), and the world actually looked in pretty good shape.

Much had changed since Cathy's visit. We now corresponded weekly, sharing our thoughts and describing activities. Her short, carefully written letters boosted my spirits. They also revealed something about her life as a Peace Corps nurse.

After visiting me, she'd had a scary experience while returning to Mbeya: The driver of her bus, who had innocently stopped to aid a victim of a hit-and-run accident, escaped being badly beaten or killed by enraged villagers only when, at the last moment, like the U.S. cavalry, the police arrived with flashing lights and whooping sirens. *Need I say I was happy to see Mbeya again?*

She lived in a small stone house shaded by cypress, pine, and eucalyptus trees on the grounds of the Mbeya hospital. It was a quiet place: passersby were few and the hospital was far enough away to be out of sight and sound. After work, Cathy liked to relax on the steps of the house beside a six-foot poinsettia … *playing soothing music on my tape recorder, or just listening to the steady hum of bees and drone of distant trucks climbing the hill to Mbeya.*

The house, condemned as unsafe for habitation, was still used because of a shortage of housing. It did have running water, however, and (unlike mine) electricity, although this sometimes didn't work. *On these occasions, I dine by candlelight.* Each cold season, a swarm of bees, seeking warmth, invaded the house where they congregated in the attic just above the water heater in the bathroom. Until the warm season returned, Cathy bathed to the hum of the hive and remembered to wear shoes around the house. She hadn't the first year, and had paid the price; each morning she encountered—often painfully—a score of bees on the floor.

Cathy had few visitors; unlike me, she didn't live at a world-renowned tourist attraction. But she didn't mind. She liked the quiet life. *I only attended the Ambassador's tea party to keep up appearances.* Still, she was thrilled to sit at the head table when Robert and Ethyl Kennedy paid a visit to the Peace Corps volunteers at Mbeya.

Cathy oversaw a women's ward in the Mbeya Government Hospital, directing the work of African nurses and male attendants who tended to sick *wananchi* (literally, people of the land). It was a free hospital, so the wards were always full; overflow patients slept on the floor. The work had its good moments. For instance, each ward had patients who were singers of religious hymns. Two old women, in particular, liked to sing along with the radio broadcasts of Swahili music. One sang so loudly that she often drowned out the radio. The other only did two songs—the TANU Party song and "Goodbye President Nyerere"—but compensated by animatedly bouncing up and down on her bed in rhythm to the tune. Another woman insisted on dancing to the music with movements so vigorous and provocative that her covering sheet threatened to fall off. *Luckily, Dennis, it's a women's ward, so no men are around.*

Sometimes Cathy just sat with her patients and contentedly watched the day roll by. Mostly, however, she spent weeks at a time rushing about, often to no avail, or so it seemed. She especially hated the times when relatives came, wailing and crying, to collect the bodies of dead patients who would have lived if the hospital was better run and the sterilizer worked, or the proper drug was available, or the doctor came when needed. *It's just so sad. Sometimes, I wish I wasn't even here!* She spent the evenings of those days writing to travel agencies.

Then Cathy was asked to join a special medical safari project. She jumped at the chance. For two weeks she bounced over rough roads in dusty Land Rovers, slept in tents, worked ten-hour days, and subsisted on orange squash, bacon, and spaghetti (unless one of the men shot a gazelle). She loved every minute of it.

Afterward, she transferred to Mpwapwa, a small town in central Tanganyika. Upon arriving she found her government-provided house already occupied by an African nurse with a five-month-old baby and eight-year-old sister. But Cathy fit right in. *You should see me now, bouncing young Humphrey on my knee while stirring the charcoal fire and eating ugali and meat with the rest of the crowd. Humphrey shadows me everywhere about the house; he's very curious. I rather like it here.*

Now that our two-year stints with the Peace Corps were drawing to a close, I wanted to secure our relationship before going on leave (we had extended our tours for another year). I had visited Cathy in Mbeya a few months earlier. Getting there had taken two days, and I'd gotten so covered with mud while helping to extricate a mired bus that I arrived looking almost as dark as the other passengers. But Cathy gave me a warm welcome and made it clear that her feelings for me hadn't changed. Then she did so again by moving to Mpwapwa, which halved the distance between us. I decided to go to Mpwapwa and propose marriage. But instead of taking a bus, I rode a motorbike.

After a two-day (twice as long as expected), butt-numbing, bone-jarring ride over three hundred miles of densely corrugated road (the motorbike vibrating like a jackhammer over every bump), I arrived at Mpwapwa feeling like my rear end had fallen off hours ago. But despite my dusty, bedraggled appearance and a tendency, when moving about, to look like a constipated duck, Cathy approved of my suggestion that we marry, which made me so happy that I felt no pain on my return to Ngorongoro. I was so bemused by my good fortune that I don't remember that part of the trip at all, not even the accident. (Dad reminded me about the accident years later. "Don't you remember losing control of the bike and crashing?" he asked. "You wrote that you sailed head first over the handlebars and that the crash broke the bike's fork. Your mother and I wondered how you managed to get home.")

Now that we were engaged, I awaited Cathy's letters with even greater anticipation. She still liked her new posting but had applied for a transfer to the hospital in Arusha. If this was approved, she would be only a hundred miles away and we would see one another more often. Staring dreamily out the window, I decided that I liked being engaged. Then, noticing I was still holding Cathy's letter, I decided to read the more-affectionate parts of it again. Broken-down bulldozers could wait.

Dear Dennis ...

The Empakaai Crater Safari

"**Herman,** look over there!" I yelled, trying to make myself heard over the noise of the airplane's engine. "That's Empakaai!" Below us, deep forested canyons sliced their way down the eastern slopes of Lolmalasin Mountain and through the Great Rift Escarpment. Kerimasi, an inactive volcano marking the northernmost point of the Crater Highlands, rose ahead of us fifteen miles away. However, our destination was Empakaai, a large cratered mountain a few miles to the southwest of Kerimasi. Herman had yet to see it.

But first we had to gain enough altitude to make it over the crater's rim the lowest part of which exceeds nine thousand feet. Increasing the revolutions of the Cessna's engine, the pilot pulled back on the controls and we began, slowly, to climb. Moving northwestward now, we watched the landscape below us change: forest becoming bush, canyons becoming shallow, ridge tops broadening. Lolmalasin dropped behind, revealing the high grassy plateau to its west. As the outer slopes of Empakaai slid beneath the plane, we began to see *bomas* and herds of livestock. The closer we approached, the faster the mountain rose to meet us. Then, suddenly, the ground dropped precipitously away as we swept over the crater rim.

Into a little bit of paradise: The crater was four miles wide and one to three thousand feet deep. The rim was actually higher than we were on some sides, so we had the sensation of flying inside a gigantic teacup. Dark green forest mantled much of the steep inner walls. Charming grassy glades lay dreaming within the forest. A lovely lake, its jade green waters fringed with a pink necklace of densely packed flamingos, smiled up from the crater floor. As we circled above, the necklace began to unravel as the large birds broke away, flying low across the water in coral-colored strands.

But now we also saw evidence of man's activities, especially on the crater floor where the forest had been destroyed. It had been replaced by an uninspiring cover of shrubs and grasses, their buff and gray, dry season colors contrasting strongly with the greenish hues of lake and forest. *Bomas* and farms scattered across the crater floor were eyesores in this otherwise beautiful setting. They also were indicators of a potential ecological hazard, for fires set (for whatever purpose) by people living on the crater floor could escape and destroy the forest on the steep crater walls.

From the way he scowled and shook his head as he surveyed the scene, Herman shared my feelings. Furthermore, knowing him, I suspected he would corner the conservator at the first opportunity and demand he do something. Well, I had good news for him. These *bomas* and fields were abandoned. The people had been forcibly removed a few months earlier by the Ngorongoro Conservation Unit and settled elsewhere.

It was an interesting story and object lesson in the modern politics of conservation. And it happened in an exceptional setting. Empakaai rises amidst some grand scenery. The view from its north rim is especially striking. Two nine-thousand-foot peaks, Gelai and Oldoinyo Lengai—the latter an active volcano—rise in stark isolation out of the flat Rift Valley floor. Lake Natron, a major breeding site for flamingos, stretches away to Kenya, its soda flats glinting whitely in the sun. Then there is Empakaai itself, with its steep forested walls, deeply set lake, and flamingos. Therefore, it wasn't surprising that the Ngorongoro Conservation Unit felt Empakaai Crater should be protected as part of Tanganyika's national heritage.

For several years, Warusha, who were farmers as well as herdsmen, and close relatives of the Maasai, had been settling in the northern Crater Highlands, including Empakaai Crater. It was illegal to live in the crater or to farm even on the outer slopes, but the Warusha paid no heed. Possibly they thought it unlikely the government would ever do anything about it. They were, after all, some distance from Ngorongoro, and much of that way was rough and had no roads.

Henry Fosbrooke had removed settlers from Empakaai Crater before, but they always came back. He also had been unable to stop farming outside the crater. However, willing to try persuasion one last time, he sent Solomon ole Saibull, then a senior assistant conservator, to the Empakaai area to speak with the Warusha. Anthony Mgina accompanied Solomon to help with the *barazas* (meetings). John Goddard and a game scout joined the safari to look for signs of rhino. A forest guard and I took the opportunity to inspect the northernmost boundary of the Northern Highlands Forest Reserve, which lay not far to the south of Empakaai Crater. Daniel came along to do the cooking. Twelve porters carried our gear. It was quite a safari.

We set out one hot November morning, twenty-one people and their gear stuffed into three Land Rovers. Crossing Ngorongoro's crater floor, we ascended to the Lemala Road on the other side, and turned northward toward Nainokanoka. This put us onto a high grassy plateau, about four to eight miles wide, which extends all the way to the upper slopes of Empakaai Mountain fifteen miles to the north.

The dirt track, roughened by numerous cattle trails and the collapsed tunnels of mole-rats, was bone jarringly bumpy. Therefore, we made slow progress into Nainokanoka, a loosely arranged collection of five wooden buildings (four government structures and a *duka*) and three Maasai *bomas*, near where the Munge River exits Olmoti Crater.

Some of us wanted to buy things we had forgotten to get at Ngorongoro, such as matches or small packets of Omo soap powder, so we stopped at the *duka*, the proprietor of which was a jolly-looking Indian with rosy cheeks and a large handle bar mustache. I waited outside, listening to the high-pitched voices of children reciting their lessons in the schoolhouse across the way. Several goats wandered by. Two warmly blanketed Maasai elders, one with a wide-brimmed hat like those worn by American Indians in the late 19th century, regarded me with interest from the *duka's* porch. Otherwise, little was happening at Nainokanoka, even at the dispensary where people should have been lining up to have their various ailments treated. Anthony Mgina, emerging from the *duka* with a small tin of Blue Band margarine in his hand, explained:

"There is no *dawa* [medicine]," he explained unhappily. "The Ministry of Health is so poor that its dispensaries often lack supplies, especially rural ones like this."

"So what happens when the people get sick?"

"They buy *dawa* from the *dukas* or from people who travel from *boma* to *boma* selling pills and giving injections—people who have no training whatsoever! They often cheat the Maasai by giving injections of water, which they call penicillin!"

The track, such as it was, ended at Nainokanoka. From there we drove across the grassland. This part of the plateau, framed on three sides by Lolmalasin, Empakaai, and Olmoti Mountains, and including the Embulbul Depression in the southeast, was a lonely place. Only a few wild animals—wildebeest, kongoni, and Grant's gazelle—and scattered herds of livestock animated the landscape. Seeing us coming, young herd boys left their animals to race into position along our route of travel. As we slowly bumped by, the kids, sometimes solemn and staring, but most often smiling and friendly, raised their right hands, palms out in salute. It looked like we were being blessed.

Reaching the lower southern slope of Empakaai, we passed through a group of Maasai *bomas*, low windowless huts squatting amidst accumulations of animal dung behind fences of cedar posts. The cedar had been cut from forested canyons three or four miles away. The inhabitants excitedly turned out to watch us drive by. They laughed and joked and peered with open mouths into our vehicles, making quite a thing of it. Cars seldom, if ever, came here.

It was getting late, so we didn't stop. Leaving the settlement behind, we drove on, passing a listless, half-starved dog with an engorged tick swelling blackly on its neck, some resting goats, a scattering of animal bones gleaming whitely in the grass, and a donkey that forced us to detour when it wouldn't move out of our way. A few hundred yards from the settlement, a cluster of abandoned *bomas*, colonized by a lush growth of grasses and weeds (stinging nettles and poisonous, white-flowered datura not very nice ones, either), stood out boldly green against an otherwise drab-colored landscape. At this point our noisy escort of Maasai children, women, and a few *murran* dropped away, and we started bumping and thumping our way across the tussocky grassland again.

Following an old cattle track that ran diagonally up a slope so steep the Land Rovers listed dangerously sideways, we reached the edge of the grassland, pushed our way through a wide belt of sagebrush-like artemesia shrubs, and found ourselves on the rim of Empakaai Crater. Far below, viewed through a frame of lichen-draped hagenia trees, lay a beautiful lake, its green waters edged in pink by thousands of flamingos massed in bands running parallel to the shore, like foamy crests of waves in the surf. The view decided us: we would camp here.

As we hurried to set up camp, the air grew cold. Thunderstorms moved restlessly over the arid plain beyond the escarpment to the east. In the evening, a succession of dark squalls swept in over the rim.

Then the flamingos left the lake's surface to spiral higher and higher, only to turn and gradually descend again. But during the next two nights, great "V's" of the long-necked birds, dimly visible in the clear moonlight, flew low, eastward out of the crater, drawing attention to their passage with croaks and ducklike peeps. They were on their way to Ngorongoro, said our men, whence they would return in a few days. Many stayed behind, however, because every morning hundreds could be seen scattered like measles over the water.

We stayed three nights, and as the elevation was about nine thousand feet, they were cold nights. John and I shared a small tent, while Solomon and Anthony, enjoying their perks of office, had a considerably larger tent as well as folding chairs, clean sheets, and a radio. They even wore pajamas. The fourteen men doing the carrying and cooking had two big tents between them.

A chilly wet fog ruled the early mornings, which we spent wrapped in blankets huddled by the fire drinking our breakfast of milky tea from tin cups. By 8 a.m., however, the fog was gone. The days were sunny and hot until late afternoon, when scattered small storms began to gather, muttering and grumbling, to cool the air, stir the wind, and send down dark slanting pillars of rain. Evenings found us once more sitting around the fire, our shoulders blanketed against the cold mountain air, talking politics.

Solomon and Anthony were patriotic Tanganyikans and, like their government, socialists. They welcomed the expropriation of the large European and Indian-owned farms then underway, and were deeply suspicious of the USA, which they suspected of being involved in a recent attempt by elements of the Tanganyika army to overthrow the government. Therefore we argued, but especially about the intentions of the United States. My earnest attempts to convince the two African gentlemen that my country—that bastion of democracy and freedom—would never countenance the overthrow of a democratically elected government (which I believed at the time) were to no avail;

their suspicions remained, although, they assured me, these did not apply to me.

"We know you, Dennis. It is your government that worries us."

(I heard that a lot.)

During the next two days Solomon and Anthony held *barazas*, or meetings with the local Warusha cultivators at Ngopironi, on the lower eastern flank of Empakaai. While they were busy I inspected the forest reserve boundary, which was about three miles south of the camp. That is, I did after I finally found it—the forest guard had to ask a local person to guide us there. Besides the forest guard and *his* guide, I had the company of John and Sambegi, the game scout, who were along to look for signs of rhino.

We finally found the boundary on the crest of a high ridge, the southern side of which dropped abruptly away into a canyon so deep and steep sided that I couldn't imagine how anyone could get across. Our guide agreed. "*Hatuwezi kupita!*" he declared. We cannot pass! Furthermore, he added, there were several similar canyons beyond this one, some of which had not been entered for generations. When the people from this area wanted to visit relatives farther to the south, they descended the escarpment, walked past the mouths of the canyons where they debouched onto the plain, and then climbed back up again. Well, that was fine with me, because it meant that here, at least, the forest reserve was safe from illegal entry. Just as well, too, because the boundary was only poorly marked by a few widely spaced wooden "beacons" resembling upended broom sticks, and seldom patrolled, as evidenced by the forest guard's inability to even find it.

On our way back to camp we found some signs of rhino. John immediately perked up. "Fantastic! Must be more than one animal in this area. Bloody good!" However, he also developed a bad case of blistered feet, which was to plague him for the rest of the trip, and I,

A view of Lake Emakat and the active volcano Oldoinyo Lengai from the south rim of Empakaai Crater. The trees are *Hagenia abyssinica*. (Photo by George Frame.)

having apparently over exhausted myself, became sick—real wimps, the both of us. That night I didn't argue politics.

On the morning of the third day we broke camp, loaded up the porters and, leaving our vehicles behind, walked through broken country covered with dry forest and scrub. We were headed for the Kapenjiro area, six or seven miles farther east, on the slopes of Mt. Kerimasi. Another *baraza* was to be held with the Warusha living there. After that, we would finally enter Empakaai Crater. Our safari resembled an expedition of exploration you read about in hunting memoirs of the 19th century: porters filing down the trail, balancing luggage on their heads; the game scout, his jaunty red beret lending color to the scene, swinging along with his rifle over his shoulder; and the senior staff—Solomon, Anthony, John and I—taking up the rear. I figured then that this was as close as I would ever get to a real foot safari, roads now being so ubiquitous in East Africa that safaris almost always were by vehicle. And I was right: I never went on another.

The trail was wide and dusty and littered with livestock droppings. It looked heavily used, as did the forest through which it passed. To be truthful, the forest looked pretty scruffy. The trees were poor specimens, and there weren't very many of them. I could see why this area wasn't in the forest reserve. Therefore I paid it little attention and, instead, entered into a discussion (well, actually more of an argument) with Solomon about the relative merits of our respective footgear—my wool socks and hiking boots versus his thin-soled penny loafers and the kind of socks worn by executives to board meetings. Amiably contending with one another, we tromped across dry pebbly creek beds overhung by large fig trees, through stands of croton and olive, past herds of sheep and goats. We overtook a Maasai woman taking a donkey loaded with metal jerry cans to a spring to get water. Two *murran* passed us going the opposite direction, walking with long, swinging, distance-eating strides.

About halfway to Kapenjiro, we came to a clearing where we stopped to rest. The porters dumped their loads, extracted crumpled packets of Sportsman and Kali cigarettes from their pockets, and sprawled on the grass to have a smoke. (*Kali* means "sharp-edged, fierce, mean, or cruel," so you can imagine what the cigarettes, which came in small green and white packets, tasted like.) The clearing commanded a striking view to the south, where roughly twenty miles of the Great Rift escarpment had been chopped and sliced into deep, steep-sided canyons. A large eagle, or perhaps a vulture—it was too far away to be certain—soared and wheeled on an updraft of warm air high above the nearest chasm.

Tiring of the view and of watching John straining with his binoculars to identify the circling, floating bird, Solomon nudged me and pointed eastward.

"Dennis, there lies Engaruka!"

Noticing the quizzical expression on my face, Solomon explained. Engaruka, he said, was an archeological site at the foot of the escarpment about five miles away, where, for over four hundred years, an unknown people—several thousand, in seven large villages—had irrigated crops from streams flowing from the highlands. Inexplicably they had vanished about two hundred years ago, leaving behind circular hut foundations cut into the hillsides; stone canals, walls, and terraced embankments; and a type of pottery completely unknown elsewhere in the region.

Fascinating: a mysterious, vanished people. What had happened to them? Where had they—

"Come on, Mr. Trees, you can dream later!" yelled one of the porters. I hadn't noticed the porters get to their feet, hump their loads onto their heads, and set out again; the front end of the column had already disappeared into the bush. Anyway, the fate of the Engaruka people was probably something less than romantic. For all I knew, some of their descendants were with us that day. Maybe the guy who yelled at me was one of them. I would deal with him later.

Our camp at Kapenjiro was a single tent shared by the four senior officers in a grassy field near several Warusha *bomas*. The afternoon air was hot, and the flies, which bred in the dung piles of the nearby *bomas,* numerous. However, the people were hospitable, bringing us water from a nearby stream, giving us a goat to slaughter for our meal, and letting our porters sleep in their *bomas,* all the while knowing that we had come to tell them to stop farming or to move. I commented on their good manners.

"But this is how the Warusha always treat their guests," Solomon exclaimed.

Anthony Mgina looked up from wiping dust from his spectacles. "Bwana, other tribes do the same, you know." Indeed, he belonged to one of them.

"Yes, of course, that is so," Solomon quickly—and surprisingly—

agreed. However, he then showed his true colors by trying to pick an argument with a sleepy- looking porter sitting nearby. In a loud, carrying voice he exclaimed, "Except for the Wambulu!" The porter, however, knew Solomon's ways. He just grinned. Then he stretched out on the grass and went to sleep.

Having arrived at Kapenjiro too late to do anything else, we spent the rest of the day there, John and I sitting around swatting flies (which the Africans just ignored) and taking photos of the Warusha. The women were very coy about being photographed. Thinking things might go easier if one of their own was involved, I preset the focus and f-stop before giving my camera to a *murrani,* who spent the next half hour or so enthusiastically chasing down and cornering squealing females. Then, as they cowered in mock horror, he pointed the camera while I reached over his shoulder and snapped the pictures. He and I had a lot of fun pounding to and fro among the huts in pursuit of giggly women, but we took some lousy photos—they were all overexposed.

Although wary of our cameras, the Warusha were drawn to John's binoculars like iron filings to a magnet. Everyone wanted to look through them, and laugh, and exclaim in wonder at seeing things appear so near which they knew to be far away. Some, while intently peering through the binoculars, even reached out to touch the objects, such as a tree on the far side of the field, which the glasses had brought so near. Such magic it was. For our part, we were amused—and touched.

Meanwhile, dust devils, some of them hundreds of feet high, swirled about the parched surface of the plain below. Eventually the sky darkened and gave birth to rain squalls which swept in over the escarpment, thundering warnings and trailing slanting walls of rain. Rain would beat heavily on the tent and the wind would whip and flap the canvas about before the storms moved on, leaving in their wake an atmosphere cleansed of dust. Distant features—dry steam beds, low hills, patterns of vegetation, a dirt road—once obscured by the haze now were clearly visible. The plain still looked arid and dry, but the dust devils were gone.

That night, while we ate goat meat roasted over the fire, Solomon ole Saibull told us how his tribe, the Warusha, had originated from elements of the Kisongo, the principal subtribe of the Maasai, who had, a few hundred years ago, pushed the agricultural Wameru people off their land on Mt. Meru and subsequently became farmers themselves.

Then, Solomon told us something even more interesting. The Kisongo had defeated another sub tribe of the Maasai, the Lumbwa, for possession of the Crater Highlands. The decisive battle had taken place on the rim of Empakaai Crater.

"What happened to the defeated warriors?" John asked.

Solomon shrugged. "What do you think? They were thrown over a cliff."

We returned next day to our original camp on the rim of Empakaai. The following morning, Solomon, Anthony, and the game scout set off into Empakaai Crater to hold the final *baraza* of the safari, this time with the Warusha who were illegally settled on the crater floor. I tagged along as a spectator, as did John, despite his raw feet (when looking for rhinos, he was a determined man).

Following a trail of sorts, we carefully climbed down the inner wall—so steep that in places we had to clutch at tree branches and rock outcrops to keep our balance—to the crater floor, which we reached about half an hour later. There we entered a dense forest. Quietly making our way among trees with smooth, gray boles, we gradually became aware of what sounded like the distant croaking of thousands of frogs. Then, abruptly, the forest ended, and we emerged into the open to see before us the crater's lake, which Solomon said was called Lake Emakat. It was full of birds. There were many ducks and shore birds, but our eyes were quickly drawn to the flamingos—big pink birds with carmine red bills, identified by John as lesser flamingos—

massed densely near shore. And, coming off the lake, louder and more pervasive than before, was that croaking we'd been hearing, the sound of thousands of lesser flamingos.

Encountering an old man herding cattle in the lush green grassland bordering the lake, we asked for directions, but he proved less friendly and cooperative than the Warusha with whom we had so far dealt. However, after several minutes of argument, Solomon again carried the day, and the old man grumpily gave in and agreed to show us where to go.

After a few minutes' walk, during which we passed several herds of cattle guarded by small boys, we came to a clearing near some *bomas*, where the old man left us while he went off to spread the news of our arrival. We waited. Over the next half hour, the elders with whom Solomon and Anthony wanted to speak appeared in one's and two's, stalking with straight-backed dignity into the clearing where they settled to the ground, squatting before us in readiness for the meeting. Like their compatriots at Kapenjiro and Ngopironi, they wore loose-fitting sheets of rust-colored *Amerikani* cloth, knotted like togas over one shoulder but leaving the other shoulder bare. Some had wrapped a second cloth or blanket (also rust-colored from long periods of soap-free use) around their shoulders. Each wore a necklace of beads and a narrow metal bracelet, and carried a yard-long stick used for walking, pointing, beating donkeys, and emphasizing points during a discussion. Four were bald. They resembled well-smoked Buddhist monks.

The *baraza* was duly held. Like most *barazas* I ever attended, there was an excess of talking, in my opinion, with everyone having his say over and over again—talk, talk, talk. John felt the same way, so he and I returned to the lake to take photographs of the flamingos and look for rhino sign along the water's edge. As we walked along the shore, our ears filled with the croaks and honks of multitudinous birds, the flamingos nearest us hurriedly peeled away from the massed flocks, awkwardly splashed through the shallow water on stilt-like legs, then soared aloft in sudden gracefulness—a stream of fluid pink against the green backdrop of forest on the crater walls—out over the lake, then back to shallow water near the shore again, where they landed a safer distance from us. Without my telephoto lens I never got close enough to take a good photo. John, of course, took a great many.

We found no rhino sign whatsoever.

"Didn't expect to," John groused from a log where he was sitting. "Not with all these people living here. They probably speared the last one years ago."

Two ducks whistled overhead, banked tightly over the lake and splashed down, startling a coot that sprinted rapidly away—running on top of the water, flapping its wings to get airborne.

"The *murran* do it just for fun you know," he added sourly.

Returning to the *baraza*, we could tell from our colleagues' stony faces and the behavior of the Warusha elders—angry people look and sound the same in any language—that our side was not doing well. Anthony and Solomon were meeting with determined resistance. Unlike the previous *barazas* held outside the crater which had ended with grudging agreements to stop farming, the Empakaai Warusha were categorically declaring their intention to stay in the crater and farm, whether the Ngorongoro Conservation Unit liked it or not. Worse yet, a number of warriors, whose job it was to settle differences of opinion violently, had gathered a few hundred feet away and were becoming increasingly restive (Solomon later said that they had been told to arm themselves and resist us if necessary). Excited shouts, and the *thump, thump, thump,* of dancing *murran* working themselves into a fighting lather, gave menace to the deliberations of the *baraza*.

Taking John and me aside, Anthony and Solomon informed us about the lack of progress and increasing hostility. There was nothing to gain by prolonging the discussion, and a great deal to lose by using threats—our total armament consisted of Sambegi's rifle and three bullets. They were ending the *baraza*. Solomon didn't like losing arguments. As we began our walk back to camp, he turned to Anthony and angrily declared, "The next time we will bring police. We will bring many and they will be well-armed."

Roughly an hour later, puffing with exertion, we reached the crater rim where John flopped to the ground with a great sigh and refused to budge for several minutes. "Wouldn't do that again even for a rhino!" he groaned. Removing his shoes and socks, he tenderly checked the soles of his feet. They looked bad.

We set off to meet the rest of our party. They had stayed behind to pack up camp and get the cars loaded in preparation for returning to Ngorongoro. Although it was no longer sunny, clouds having formed overhead while we were in the crater, our spirits rose. After several days of walking, we looked forward to resting our tired feet in a car, no matter how bumpy the ride might be. Also, the packing was probably not done yet, so there would be time for tea. Like horses headed for the stables, we quickened our steps toward camp—only to find it had vanished. There were no people, no tents, and no vehicles. Only flattened grass where the tents had stood, some oil spots where the vehicles had been parked, and the smoldering remains of two campfires remained. The entire group—seventeen men—had packed up and left without us.

Solomon and Anthony exchanged incredulous looks. Then Solomon exploded. "Who gave these … these *people* permission to leave without us?" he demanded, his eyes bulging in anger. John, who had fallen behind once again, limped painfully into the clearing. Stopping short, he stared blankly at the empty camp site. Then, comprehension arrived. "There's nobody here!" he exclaimed. "They've gone and taken everything with…. My car—*Where's my Land Rover!*"

View from the rim of Empakaai Crater southwest across highland grassland and the Embulbul Depression to Oldeani Mountain in the far distance. Olmoti Crater is on the right. Well-worn cattle trails are in the foreground.

Then it started raining.

We followed the path of crushed grass and broken shrubs left by the vehicles to the edge of the open grassland on the southern slopes of Empakaai Mountain. Using his binoculars, John finally spied them: the vehicles were parked beside some Maasai *bomas*, over a mile away, at the edge of the Embulbul Depression.

"They have gone to drink milk," Sambegi announced with a broad grin.

"Anthony, we must speak with these people," Solomon declared with a grim smile.

With that, the two of them set off purposefully down the hill toward the *bomas*.

When John, Sambegi, and I finally reached the *bomas*, we saw from the sheepish expressions on the men's faces that the two bosses, who had arrived well ahead of us, had spoken sharply to them about their unauthorized departure from camp. In contrast, Solomon was looking quite chipper: a dust-up with the rank and file had improved his day no end. We found him next to a *boma* gate drinking from a large gourd. "*Karibu maziwa*," he called out, inviting us to come drink some milk.

Gratefully collapsing into the Land Rovers, we set off homeward across the high plateau, leaving cloud-shrouded Empakaai (and the rain) behind. Slowly we bumped our way over tussocks of wire grass, returning the waves (but not the whistles) of cheerful herd boys. Larks flitted about in the sun, and a soft, warm breeze flowed in through open windows. But our respite was to be brief because, four or five miles ahead, clouds were forming over Olmoti and Ngorongoro Craters. Soon the sky before us turned charcoal black with falling rain, and we heard the low grumble of distant thunder. We were in for a wet trip home.

The inhabitants of Empakaai Crater were removed in December, 1965, by a detachment of the Tanganyika Police Field Force.

A Serengeti Game Count

It was nearing noon as our four-seat Cessna aircraft *brrrrrred* its way along, three hundred feet above the eastern Serengeti Plains. The small plane bumped, swayed, slid, and jiggled. Updrafts of sun-warmed air jostled it about. It unexpectedly dropped into air pockets. Abrupt shifts in the wind pushed it this way and that. We were nearly finished with the aerial census and I, for one, couldn't wait to get back on the ground.

In contrast, our takeoff from the small dirt strip on the floor of Ngorongoro Crater was silky smooth in the cool, stable, early morning air. It took us directly over the shallow, muddy water of Lake Makat, where flamingos feeding along the lake's fringe skittered nervously at the plane's racing shadow. Circling higher and higher over the crater, we eventually gained enough altitude to clear the crater rim and allow the pilot to set course towards the Serengeti Plains, now visible to the northwest. The plane bumped a bit in an updraft as we passed over the crater rim, but quickly settled down again: it was too early in the day to encounter seriously rough air. Now we could see the western flanks of the Crater Highlands, corrugated with shallow, shadow-filled canyons, sloping away before us toward the Serengeti Plains, and the long east west gash of Oldupai Gorge. The plains filled the entire windshield of the airplane.

Upon reaching the plains we turned south. Herman Dirschl, sitting in front, conferred with the pilot about the flight plan for the day's aerial census. This was the first day of the census which was to estimate population densities of wildlife and livestock species within the Ngorongoro Conservation Area—information necessary for Herman's Management and Development Plan. In return for Herman's helping me with mapping vegetation, I was assisting him with the census. Philip, sitting beside me in the back seat, completed our team.

We were not into position yet so I relaxed and soaked up impressions. The grassy plain was tinted a soft yellowish orange by the early morning light. An occasional acacia tree streaked the grassland with its long, narrow shadow. Some wildlife was beginning to appear: A startled rhino trotted from a thicket of sansevieria as we roared overhead; a giraffe looked up inquisitively from the lonely shrub it was browsing; a small, graceful Thomson's gazelle bounced away from us across the grass. Then Herman, who had been closely following our progress on his map, said, "*Now!*" The pilot nodded and banked the plane into a turn as, in the back seat, Philip and I quickly adjusted our viewing positions and turned on our tape recorders. The census had begun.

"*Four wildebeest*" ... "*Tommy*" ... "*Two ostrich*" ... "*Rhino*" ..., Philip and I spoke into our tape recorder mikes as we recorded animals seen within census strips marked by two fiberglass fishing rods taped to each strut of the high-winged plane. "*Twenty zebra*" ... "*Wildebeest*" ... "*Six eland*" ... "*Fifteen wildebeest*" ..., (*Click*—groups of more than twenty animals were photographed). Back and forth across the lush, animal-dotted plains we droned.

It was the rainy season and the eastern portion of the Serengeti Plains lying within the Ngorongoro Conservation Area was hosting the Serengeti migrations. Hundreds of thousands of hoofed herbivores, guided by distant rain storms, had wended their way there through miles of thorn bush to graze the new green grass and have their calves. The herds contain many zebra and Thomson's gazelle, but it is the sheer numbers of wildebeest that define the migrations. During the rainy season, the Serengeti is Wildebeest Country.

Wildebeest form herds so dense it sometimes seems you could walk for miles on their backs without touching the ground. They scatter across the gently undulating landscape so that everywhere you look, there are wildebeest. They form grazing fronts up to a thousand animals wide as they crop their way across the plains, like a huge lawn mower. They thunder across the road in front of cars much like bison once did in front of locomotives in North America. They playfully caper. They peacefully graze. They lie down and doze. They file away in lines up to four miles long to go somewhere else.

Then, seemingly overnight, the emerald plains are full of fawn-colored calves wobbling on unsteady feet. They can, within an hour, run beside their mothers on long gangly legs. Indeed, they must do so, or risk being taken by predators—lion, cheetah, wild dog, hyena, jackal—that prowl through the herds searching for the very young, the sick, the lost, and the unwary. However, something else helps them survive—they simply overwhelm the predators. So many thousands arrive over such a short time, that the predators just can't keep up.

"Six cattle" … *"Nine"* … *"Fifteen"* … Near the southern edge of the plains, we passed over fields of bright yellow flowers carpeting Ildonyo Hill (from a distance, they had appeared as a red mirage). Now, instead of wildebeest and zebra, we saw cattle, brought here by their Maasai owners to keep them from grazing grass contaminated by the afterbirth of wildebeest calves, which has something in it that causes cattle to sicken and die. *"Ten cows"* … *"Three"* … *"Twenty"* … *"Two kongoni"* … *"Four wart hog"* …

As we passed over Oldupai Gorge for the first time, I looked up from my animal-counting duties and saw our pilot pouring coffee into a cup from a thermos flask. He was as nonchalant as if he were at the breakfast table, rather than in an airplane speeding along only a few hundred feet above the ground. I briefly wondered if that was a wise thing to do, but then returned to counting animals. Two minutes later, the plane went berserk. Like a rodeo bull trying to dislodge an especially adhesive cowboy, it proceeded to go up, down, and sideways, all at the same time—we had encountered the first turbulence of the day. The pilot yelped as the coffee cup, which had been resting on the dashboard of the plane, rose into the air and emptied its contents down his front. He spent the next several seconds struggling to get the plane under control. The remainder of the flight was spent *sans* coffee.

Oldupai Gorge was a major rhino study area for John Goddard who often scouted through its thorny acacia and commiphora trees and sharp-tipped sansevieria looking for the big beasts. A few months earlier, he, Pat Hemingway, and I had tried to census them from the air. (Pat, an instructor at the Mweka College of Wildlife Management near Moshi, was an amiable man with a window-shattering laugh, and a disinclination to talk about his famous father, so we never did.) In between rhino sightings—we found eighteen that trip—John pointed out where, on earlier visits to Oldupai, he had fallen from a tree into a patch of sansevieria (*that*, he assured us, had *hurt*); encountered a pride of lions at close quarters while walking with Richard Leakey (luckily, the lions didn't attack); and stood in the upper branches of a large tree, watching with amusement as a rhino, which knew he was somewhere nearby, circled the tree looking for him.

That flight was done during the height of the dry season. Large areas of the nearby Crater Highlands lay blackened by grass fires, two of which were still smoking on the slopes of Makarut and Olmoti Mountains. The plains, although dappled with cloud shadows, and receiving the attention of a small storm (harbinger of the coming rainy season), stretched monotonously away before us, dry, brown, and seemingly devoid of life.

"*Twenty wildebeest, six, ten, four, fifteen, eight, twenty.*" [Click]. "*Ten* zebra" ... [*Click, click, click.*] It wasn't devoid of life now; rather the opposite. Everywhere, the grass lay green and lush, and small pools of rain water glinted in the sunshine. Vultures and other large birds such as storks, eagles, and kites wheeled and soared—twice, the pilot had to take evasive action to keep from hitting one—and wildebeest in their hundreds of thousands (together with at least six other herbivore and five predator species) darkened and dotted the plain. There were so many animals, we could hardly keep up. "*Four wildebeest, ten, twenty* [click, click], *five, four, six, fifteen*" ... "*Two zebra, three*" ..., we bawled into our tape recorders.

The gnus and zebras were still coming thick and fast as we flew over the site where Herman and I had camped the previous week. We had been working on the vegetation survey. For the first few days, the plains around our little camp, although nicely green, had been almost empty. Our nights were uneventful except for insects attracted to the bright light of our Petromax lantern. Indeed, it seemed to be the focal point—and incandescent Black Hole—for every insect in the entire Serengeti Plains. We could even hear the largest of our nightly visitors, dung or scarab beetles, coming as they buzzed closer and closer in the night, until suddenly they whirred in from out of the dark to bang violently against the lantern, or one of us. Every night, the ground was littered with these little flying tanks

Then, one day when we returned to camp, it was surrounded by so many animals that we had trouble finding our tents—the migrations had arrived. That night, hundreds of gnus grunted around us like amorous bull frogs, providing a background sporadically broken by the drumming hooves of frightened animals dashing past camp, and the deep-throated roars of a lion on the hill above us. The next morning we awoke, having survived the lion and being trampled by galloping wildebeest, to find that rain, which had fallen during the night, had washed down the hill, swept into our floorless tents—around which we had neglected to dig drainage ditches—and soaked everything. "*Two zebra*" ... "*Three Tommies*" ... "*Five wildebeest*" ...

On the other hand, the dune-rippled Angata Salei or Plain of the Salei (the Salei are a section of the Maasai Tribe), was, for all practical purposes, empty. So far east that it almost falls over the edge of the Great Rift escarpment north of the Crater Highlands, the Angata Salei is the easternmost part of the Serengeti Plains. Some cattle and game animals—zebra, kongoni, and Grant's gazelle—were scattered among the plain's many sand dunes—formed from ash deposits from eruptions of the volcano Oldoinyo Lengai—but none of them appeared in our survey transects. The vast herds of wildebeest that we had seen elsewhere had not yet penetrated this far

Turning in his seat, Herman yelled, "End of transect! Stop counting!" We had crossed the northern boundary of the Ngorongoro Conservation Area. But just then someone yelled, "Oryx! Look at the oryx!" and we all craned to look down at the large (up to 400 lb) striking, fawn-colored antelopes with black and white face markings and long, spear-like horns. Seeing oryx was a big deal, because they were not common. "*Choroa*," said Philip, giving us their Swahili name. "They can kill lions with those horns!"

The left wing dipped as the pilot put the plane into a tight, banking turn, filling the windows on the right side with blue sky, and those on the left with an undulating landscape of mostly grass-covered dunes that wheeled in position ninety degrees before the plane came out of its turn and leveled off again. Our next transect would begin over the Oldoinyo Gol Mountains.

The Gol Mountains almost, but not quite, wall off the Angata Salei from the rest of the Serengeti Plains. Rugged of terrain, they are several million years older than the volcanic Crater Highlands. Indeed, they *look* old. Their numerous gullies and canyons, stubble of shrubs and small thorn trees, outcrops of gneiss and quartzite rocks, and Maasai *bomas*—mostly empty and looking like ringworm along the edges of a large grassy plateau—put me in mind of an old, unshaven geezer with scalp problems.

"Oldoinyo Gol means a hard place to live," yelled Philip. "There are few springs or wells here, few reliable sources of water."

"Not many animals either," Herman hollered back, which was true because, so far, we had only seen a few small herds of livestock.

Then, suddenly, we were over the Angata Kiti, or Narrow Plain, and there below us, streaming eastward in long lines, was a veritable army of animals. We had found the migrations again. "*Ten wildebeest*" ... "*Twelve, six, fourteen*" ... "*Three zebra*" ...

Too busy counting animals, we had no time to look down the length of the Kiti Plain toward Lemuta Hill, which lies across the Angata Kiti's western entrance like a long low breakwater breasting the green swells of the Serengeti Plains. It was near Lemuta Hill that I once discovered a newborn Thomson's gazelle lying curled up in the grass where its mother had left it. The little thing was so well-camouflaged and instinctively still, I almost stepped on it. In fact, after returning to the car to get my camera, I had difficulty finding it again. That same day, I came upon a zebra colt so sick I killed it to put it out of its misery. Five minutes later, it was covered by a hissing, jostling, bouncing mass of vultures shouldering one another aside to tear at the dead body. Carcasses don't last long in the Serengeti. "*Sixteen wildebeest*" ... "*Ten zebra*" ... "*Five wildebeest*" ...

As the morning matured, senses dulled. Alertness declined. The concentrated effort not to miss anything appearing, however briefly, between those two fishing rods, began to tell. The plane's constant vibration, previously unnoticed because I was so interested in other things, was noticed now. "*Thirteen wildebeest*" ... "*Two eland*" ... "*Twenty wildebeest*" ... "*Four giraffe*"

On our next pass over Oldupai, a few miles west of the site where, in 1959, Mary Leakey discovered what was then the oldest known evidence of proto man, two tourist vehicles with their tops open for better game viewing were just crossing the gorge on the Ngorongoro-Seronera road. We were not the only ones looking at wildlife today.

"*Kongoni*" … "*Tommy*" … "*Four wildebeest*" … "*Two ostrich*" … To our left, near a tree-lined tributary of Oldupai Gorge, a vaguely S-shaped herd of a thousand or so wildebeest darkened the mottled green grassland. To our right, showing as white specks against a large grayish black rain storm near Seronera, a flock of European storks leisurely spiraled up the invisible barber pole of an updraft of warm air. Below them lay Naibardad Hill in a forest of small whistling thorn trees. I recognized the landmarks. Somewhere around here I had shot a wildebeest last year.

As an officer of the Ngorongoro Conservation Unit, I was authorized—and sometimes asked—to shoot game so that government road crews working in the bush could have meat. John Goddard and I, with the local road crew in the back of his Land Rover pickup, were driving around looking for something to shoot, when a line of wildebeest appeared, plodding eastward. I was feeling playful that day so, despite the fact that the wildebeest were a long way off—maybe four hundred yards or so—I jestingly nudged John and said, "I'll get one with my first shot!" Unfortunately, instead of grunting, "Oh sure," John stuck his head out the window and informed the men in back about this upcoming feat of marksmanship, which forced me to follow through on my boast. As the road crew jeered me on and loudly told one another that another meatless day was in the offing, I stepped from the car and, trying to look like I knew what I was doing, raised the rifle to my shoulders, aimed, and fired.

The lead animal collapsed as though its feet had been yanked out from under it. One moment it was upright and walking, and the next moment it was on the ground. We quickly drove over and found that it was dead all right, its spine severed just behind the head; the wildebeest probably hadn't felt a thing. The road crew pounded enthusiastically on the roof of the cab and yelled out compliments about my shooting;

Part of the Serengeti migrations, wildebeest and zebra scattered across the eastern Serengeti Plains. Naabi Hill, entrance to the Serengeti National Park, is in the background.

Maasai warriors watch the refueling of an airplane on the floor of Ngorongoro Crater. Photo was taken during an aerial census of wildlife and livestock in the Ngorongoro Conservation Area.

John slapped me on the back. I had dropped a wildebeest with one shot, at a distance of four hundred yards. I was not about to tell anyone that I had actually aimed at the animal behind it.

"*Ten wildebeest*" ... "*Rhino*" ... "*Three zebra*" ... "*Two Tommies*" ... Late in the morning, warm air rising from the earth's surface beneath us began bumping the plane around in earnest. "*Ten wildebeest*" ... "*Sixteen*" ... (Whump!—the plane hit an updraft.) "*Five wildebeest*" ... "*Zebra*" ... (*Uggghmfp*—we drop into an air pocket.) "*Twenty wildebeest*" ...

I began feeling odd, the sort of odd feeling that precedes being sick. So it was that the last half hour of the census wasn't much fun. However, we finally reached the end of the last transect. Herman, satisfied with the work done that morning, nodded, and the pilot put us into a turning climb back toward Ngorongoro Crater. The higher we rose in the sky, the less bumpy our ride became. Leaving the plains behind, we maintained altitude that would take us just over the crater rim. Slowly, very slowly, the outer slopes of the highlands rose beneath us until we were only about a hundred feet above the ground. Then my stomach gave an involuntary lurch as the ground below, which I happened to be intently watching at the time, abruptly dropped two thousand feet away. We had passed over the rim into the crater. Later, after the plane had landed and rolled to a stop before a scattered audience of bored wildebeest, I gingerly eased myself out the door to stand, and stretch, and marvel at how the ground managed to stay so still. I decided then that while flying can be fun, stopping can be pretty enjoyable, too.

Time to Go Home

Disbelievingly, the Chinese forester exclaimed, "You call this bamboo?" An official visitor from mainland China where, apparently, they grew the real thing, he had come to see how China's experience in bamboo culture could best be transmitted to Tanganyika (or more accurately, Tanzania, which was the nation's new name). I and Bill Carmichael, the genial regional forest officer, had driven him up the forested slopes of Oldeani Mountain to where the tall pillar wood trees, crotalaria shrubs, and grassy glades gave way to dense, tightly packed stands of smooth-stemmed bamboo. A bit farther on we stopped the car and got out. Except for an occasional distant pop and snap coming from browsing elephants, the bamboo was eerily quiet—quiet and surreal. This was not a normal forest, but a collection of tightly packed, large, leafy toothpicks.

The expert was not impressed. He was, in fact, contemptuous. He described how bamboo ought to be: thick of stem, tall of stature, fast-growing and, most of all, *used*. In China there were many uses for bamboo. Here, it seemed only to be elephant fodder.

However, he must have realized the impression he was making, because he suddenly became more congenial. This was, after all, not a bad stand of bamboo. Well, not really, he supposed. We were graciously thanked for escorting him to this, ah, attractive place. Something worthwhile would undoubtedly follow from this visit. Please, would we accept a small gift in repayment for our hospitality? Then, as we stood, a lonely trio among the silent bamboo, he took from his pocket two small but exquisitely beautiful Chinese postage stamps, one for me and one for Carmichael.

That night, after Bill and the bamboo expert returned to Arusha, I sat listening to classical music on the BBC, reviewing the day. As with so many others at Ngorongoro, it had been interesting. But I would not be experiencing such days much longer, because my time was almost up. Halfway through my third and final year—the maximum stay allowed a volunteer by the Peace Corps—I would soon have to leave, whether I wanted to or not. *It had to end sometime,* I told myself.

However, that didn't mean I was slacking off. If anything, I was busier than ever, mapping vegetation, constructing a road around the northern rim of Ngorongoro Crater, pushing another across ten miles of highlands from Nainokanoka to Empakaai Crater, and doing other things as well. The work was sometimes frustrating. Occasionally, it was frightening. However, it was seldom boring. Just within the last three months, the bulldozer flipped a log into the air and almost brained me. A week later, the same machine celebrated two and a half years of spasmodic, off-again, on-again performance by breaking down for what seemed like the nine hundred and fifty-fourth time. Twice, a Land Rover in which I was riding broke down, each time forcing me to walk several miles through buffalo-infested bush without benefit of an armed game scout. Another, moving slowly down a muddy road, skidded and turned on its side, spilling a great deal of engine oil and a number of people standing in the back onto the ground (we lifted it upright and proceeded on). High winds in the eastern Serengeti blew my tent over, breaking poles and ripping the canvas. At Munge Camp on the crater floor, I watched thirty hyenas drive a lion off its kill.

Near Nainokanoka, while walking ahead of the tractor, I had a narrow escape from a rhino.

The rhino, which, by the way, was *huge*, caught me unarmed and in the open, with nowhere to hide and nothing to climb. Unexpectedly emerging from a clump of bushes, it noted my presence, lined me up in its sights (or so it seemed), and surged across the grass at me like a rapidly accelerating steam engine. Bravely, I held my ground for all of half a second before deciding that the advice given me for such a situation—"Use a .577 caliber, old chap; stops them every time"—might not apply, whereupon I reverted to a maximum speed defensive retrograde maneuver, part way through which I tripped and fell flat on my face. This must have put me beneath the rhino's radar because, instead of goring me or enthusiastically mashing me into the grass, it steamed right past and never came back.

"*Mungu alikusaidia!*" the caterpillar driver excitedly declared as I hoisted my trembling limbs back on board. God helped you!

I could only agree.

Returning to Ngorongoro that evening, I found the Peace Corps medical team, which was to carry out a smallpox vaccination campaign among the Maasai, camping out in my back yard, the chassis of their team leader's Land Rover bent out of shape, and its generator damaged from being side swiped by a truck on the way up from Dar es Salaam. That night, while everyone congregated in my house to socialize, one of the volunteers, exhausted from driving all the way from Singida in central Tanganyika, went outside to do something, and never came back. After a frantic search we finally found him curled up sleeping in the flowerbed just a few feet from the door. It was a good thing we did because the rain really bucketed down that night. Then a few days later two female team members, one of whom was Cathy, went missing while out vaccinating Maasai. The next day, just as the search party set out to look for them, they appeared, tired, smoky, and flea-bitten, but otherwise in good shape and wondering what the fuss was all about.

Indignantly, they denied having been lost at all. They had just lingered too long at their last *boma* of the day, and had stayed the night because they didn't want to walk several miles back to camp in the dark. The *boma*'s chief elder had shooed them into his hut, together with a few special goats, and had slept across the door so that the warriors knew to stay away. "Lost! Hmmph!"

The shadows in the room flickered as an olive log burning in the fireplace suddenly flared, breaking my train of thought. From his quarters behind the house, Daniel called out "*Kwaheri*" to a departing visitor. Then silence comfortably closed in around me again, and I returned to my ruminations: Cathy—I'd been thinking about Cathy.

Happily she had managed a transfer to Arusha, only a few hours' drive from Ngorongoro. Now we saw each another more often, say every two weeks or so. The authorities had given her Jo and Judy's old house on the grounds of the government hospital. It was a small wooden structure with an avocado tree growing in the front yard, and metal window grates so thin that either there had been insufficient funds for sturdier material, or there was little risk of a burglary. Perhaps the residents of Arusha were honest types.

That they might be was fortunate, because there were many of them round, especially on the eucalyptus-shaded street in front of Cathy's house: women in colorful *kitenge* dresses, soberly attired clerks, gum booted farmers, uniformed schoolchildren, and *mashuka*-clad tribesmen. Conversations and laughter floated in over the roadside hedge, as did the warning "pings" and "trings" of bicycle bells, and lively Swahili music from hand-held radios. Even late at night, somebody was always passing by.

The proximity of Cathy's house to the hospital, the existence of one or two large gaps in the hedge separating it from the lane, and the casual attitude of Africans toward privacy led to the creation of an informal but well-worn path through her yard which passed a few feet from her bedroom. It wasn't unusual for Cathy to find her unmentionables, hung out to dry, being closely inspected by an interested African woman with a baby on her back. Young children often peered in through her bedroom window to see how the *mzungu* mama (white woman) lived. She also became accustomed, while sitting on the front porch, to having people suddenly appear from around the side of the house and, with a cheery "*Jambo*," or "*Salama*," wave to her as they walked across the front yard to disappear through one of the holes in the hedge.

Cathy's duties at the Arusha hospital differed little from those at her previous two government hospitals. The exception was that as more Europeans lived in Arusha Region, they appeared more often as patients than at Mbeya or Mpwapwa. One of the more-interesting was a Scottish wildlife biologist, Iain Douglas-Hamilton, who encountered a rhino to his disadvantage in Lake Manyara National Park. It charged, Iain tripped and fell, was trampled by the rhino, and spent several days swaddled in bandages in Arusha hospital. A few months later, he got into trouble again, this time while showing a visitor some elephants he was studying. Several of the large animals unexpectedly attacked and bashed up his Land Rover. This time, Iain (and his visitor, Katy Newlin, a Peace Corps volunteer), received only minor injuries. The Land Rover, however, was a different matter. Iain provides exciting accounts of both incidents in his and his wife Oria's interesting book, *Among the Elephants*.

Outside the house a prowling hyena whooped mournfully, waking me from my reverie. The fire which, last time I noticed, had been burning merrily away in the fireplace, was now a bed of glowing coals. The short-wave radio, having wandered off frequency, was whining and crackling with static. The feeble, slowly pulsating light from the Petromax lantern showed that it needed pumping. Again the hyena whooped, but farther away this time. I looked at my watch and realized the lateness of the hour. Turning off the lantern, I opened the door and checked for buffalo with a flashlight before making my way through the thick, cool mist (Ngorongoro was shrouded in clouds again) to the bedroom. Then, quick as I could, its being cold and all, I crawled under the covers. However, before closing my eyes, I thought of Cathy again. We were to marry in Arusha before going back to the States, but as I couldn't get into town often enough, she was making most of the wedding arrangements herself. Sleepily, I wondered how she was getting on.

A few days later, I found out.

"Do you know what I had to do for you last week?" the lady in question demanded.

Preoccupied with the way her blue stretch pants tightened in all the right places, and with the savory smell of the sausages she was frying, my response was a laggardly, "Mmm … ah, what?"

Turning away from the single-burner gas stove, she swiped strands of soft hair from her face before menacing me with a half-fried sausage impaled on a fork. "First of all," she heatedly declared, "as you weren't anywhere *around*, I had to go by *myself* to the Area Commissioner to get *our* marriage license."

"But—"

"Where I had to stand in line for forty minutes."

"You know I tried—"

"Dennis, I was the only woman there!"

"Well that should—"

"Then [she was really worked up now] when I finally reached the counter, and in front of all those African husbands-to-be lined up behind me, I had to swear—aloud, mind you—that you had no other wives. You should have seen the expression on his face, Dennis. It was *embarrassing*!"

"Uh." This was bad. I was in trouble.

Turning back to the stove, wayward strands of hair once more dangling over her eyes, Cathy resumed frying—or more accurately, stabbing—the sausages sizzling in the pan. She seemed sorry to have missed when she'd waved that fork at me.

Finally, banging down a plate of sausages on the table between us, she sat down. "Hope you like these things, because that's what we're having!"

Warily, I eyed my true love across the sausages, wondering what to do now. Finally, I speared one and began to eat.

"Say, these are good! Want some more?"

Startled, I looked up to find Cathy grinning impishly at me.

Oof! What was I getting into here?

Whatever it was, it was getting inexorably nearer. The following weekend, Cathy and I took the bus to Nairobi to buy her wedding dress and the engagement and wedding rings. That night we attended the cinema to watch *Hatari*, which features John Wayne as the leader of a team of professional wild animal-catchers working in Tanganyika. The audience, largely Africans and Indians, loved it, roaring and whistling with approval every time John Wayne spoke a few words of Kiswahili.

Back in Arusha again, I asked the Father at the Catholic Church to officiate at the wedding. I did this with some concern, because in those days, Catholic priests often refused to perform "mixed denomination" marriages. And, indeed, my worries seemed about to be confirmed when the priest, a slightly stooped, middle-aged American belonging to the White Fathers Order, began the interview by asking if Cathy and I were both Catholics.

"No, I'm not," I had to admit.

His expression sobered. There was a brief pause before the interview continued.

"But you do believe in the Holy Trinity," he said, making it a statement rather than a question.

"Er, well ..." This wasn't going well at all.

The priest hesitated again, his brow furrowed in thought, while I, certain now that the interview had failed, wondered how to break it to Cathy that the Catholic Church had rejected me as marriageable material.

"Surely you believe in God?" the white-robed father finally asked, desperate to find some redeeming quality in me.

"Yes, yes, yes," I stammered, happy to agree to something.

"Great," he exclaimed with a broad smile. "Want to see the church?"

Marriage crept closer yet.

Then one day, it arrived. The wedding was a small affair, because neither of our respective families was able to travel to Africa for it. Only friends and acquaintances attended, and the paucity of witnesses became evident when we found the entire wedding party could have been crammed into the first four rows. With a bit of care we could have fit the entire group into the living room of a normal house.

Despite the feeling that the ceremony was taking place in a small corner of an empty Grand Central Station, we proceeded anyway. Bill Carmichael, the Regional Forest Officer who, in his late fifties, was in appearance and behavior the most fatherly and distinguished looking of our colleagues, gave Cathy away; Katy Newlin, Cathy's bridesmaid, looked fetching in a red *sari*; Larry Harris, the best man, remembered to bring the wedding ring; Cathy and I said, "*I do*," at the right time and, suddenly, we were married. Following the ceremony, Bill Carmichael drove us in his big four-door, baby blue Mercedes to the house of Barry Bloom, the Peace Corps Representative, for the wedding reception, where we drank champagne, cut the wedding cake (three thick layers separated by upended wine glasses), made speeches, and took photographs. (Our official portrait photo shows a stunning beauty in a white Indian *sari* standing beside a gaunt-looking blond guy in an oversized suit. He looks relieved that *that's all over with.* Little did he know that *that* was just beginning.) Afterward, the two of us drove away in a borrowed car (not the Mercedes, unfortunately), dragging an old car door someone had tied to the back bumper, followed by honking vehicles driven some high-spirited guests, to honeymoon at Momela Lodge, where much of the movie *Hatari* had been filmed. (Who knows, maybe we even slept in John Wayne's old bed.)

Our last month with the Peace Corps was spent at Ngorongoro. Our final safari was into the highland grasslands north of Ngorongoro Crater, where fog swirled and hyenas whooped and prowled around our tent at night. Then we packed up to go home. In this we were not alone, because others at Ngorongoro also were leaving, or had already gone: the Goddards to Kenya's Tsavo National Park, where John would continue his work on rhino; the Dirschls to Canada, where Herman would head up ecological studies in the north part of the country; Oscar Charlton to retirement in England; and Philip ole Seyalel to become a warden in the Serengeti National Park. As only Solomon ole Saibull and Anthony Mgina were staying behind—despite Anthony's continuing efforts to retire—Ngorongoro would soon have an almost completely new complement of senior staff.

Ngorongoro gave me many fond memories—of monsoon clouds boiling over the eastern crater rim; olive logs burning in the fireplace on cool foggy days; cattle moving across dewy grassland in the early morning; evening shadows lengthening on the crater floor; pillar wood trees and frothy-topped bamboo; checking for buffaloes before going to bed at night. But Cathy and I knew it was time to go. We wanted to see family and friends, meet our respective in-laws for the first time, and return to school. Besides, it wasn't as though we were leaving forever, because we weren't. Texas A&M University had just awarded me a graduate assistantship to study woodland ecology in the Serengeti National Park, just next door.

We were coming back—to Tanzania. Tanganyika was no more.

Scientific Names of Selected Plant Species

Cape chestnut. *Calodendrum capense*

Cedar. *Juniperus procera*

Crotalaria. *Crotalaria imperialis*

East African camphorwood. *Ocotea usambarensis*

Fever tree. *Acacia xanthophloea*

Flamboyant. *Delonix regia*

Kikuyu grass. *Pennisetum clandestinum*

Loliondo. *Olea welwitschii*

Manyatta grass. *Eleusine jaegeri*

Mninga. *Pterocarpus angolensis*

Mexican pine. *Pinus patula*

Monterey pine. *Pinus radiate*

Mvule. *Chlorophora excelsa*

Nandi flame. *Spathodea nilotica*

Nuxia. *Nuxia congesta*

Pillar wood. *Cassipourea malosana*

Red mahogany. *Khaya nyasica*

Red oat grass. *Themeda triandra*

Red thorn. *Acacia lahai*

Star grass. *Cynodon dactylon*

Umbrella acacia. *Acacia tortilis*

Whistling thorn. *Acacia drepanolobium*

Wire grass. *Pennisetum schimperi*

Bibliography and Further Reading

Dale, I. R., and P.J. Greenway. *Kenya Trees and Shrubs.* London: Buchanan's Kenya Estates Ltd., in association with Hatchards, London, 1961.

Dorst, Jean, and Pierre Dandelot. *A Field Guide to the Larger Mammals of Africa.* London: Collins, 1970.

Douglas-Hamilton, Iain, and Oria Douglas-Hamilton. *Among the Elephants.* New York: The Viking Press, 1975.

Fosbrooke, Henry. *Ngorongoro: The Eighth Wonder.* London: Andre Deutsch, 1972.

Frame, George, and Lory Herbison Frame. *Swift and Enduring: Cheetahs and Wild Dogs of the Serengeti.* New York: E.P. Dutton, 1981.

Grzimek, Bernhard, & Michael Grzimek. *Serengeti Shall Not Die.* London: Collins, 1969.

Hayes, Harold. *The Last Place on Earth.* New York: Stein and Day Publishers, 1977.

Koenig, Oscar. *The Masai Story.* London: Michael Joseph, 1956.

Kruuk, Hans. *Hyaena.* London: Oxford University Press, 1975.

Lithgow, Tom, and Hugo van Lawick. *The Ngorongoro Story.* Nairobi: Camerapix Publishers International, 2004.

Phillipson, D.W. *The Later Prehistory of Eastern and Southern Africa.* London: Heinemann, 1977.

Saibull, Solomon ole, and Rachel Carr. *Herd and Spear: The Maasai of East Africa.* London: Collins and Harvill Press, 1991.

Glossary

Africanize. To put an African in a position once held by a European or Indian, a common occurrence in the years following independence.

Amerikani. Unbleached calico cloth, named after the American traders who introduced it to East Africa.

askari. Soldier, policeman. (Swahili words of more than one syllable stress next-to-last.)

baraza. Public meeting

boffin. Scientist, expert.

boma. Fortification, government offices, Maasai home/encampment (including huts and fenced enclosure for livestock).

buibui. Black garment that covers the body from head to foot, worn outdoors by Muslim women.

duka. Small shop

gari. Car, automobile.

hatari. Danger; also the title of a John Wayne movie set in Tanganyika in the late 1950's.

Hodi? Polite inquiry, "May I come in?" to which one answers, "*Karibu*."

Jambo. Greeting: "How do you do?"

kanga. Two-piece dress: One piece is tucked in just above the breasts and reaches to the ankle, the other is worn over the shoulders or head.

Karibu. "Come in," the correct reply to *Hodi*.

kitenge. Similar to *kanga*, but of thicker cloth.

Kwaheri. "Goodbye."

Maa. The Maasai language

mabati. Corrugated metal roofing, singular ***bati***.

mandazi. Deep-fried donut without the hole, sometimes dipped in sugar.

manyatta. Another name for a Maasai encampment

murrani. Maasai warrior, plural ***murran.***

mzungu. A white man of European extraction, plural ***wazungu.***

mzee. (Pronounced mm-ZAY.) An elder person; a term of respect.

ng'ombe. (nn-GO'm-bay.) Cow, cattle.

nyati. African or Cape, buffalo

panga. Machete

Salama. Greeting: "Good wishes."

samosa. Deep-fried, triangular pastry filled with meat, onions, and peppers.

shuka. Sheet used as loin cloth, plural ***mashuka.***

simi. A Maasai warrior's short sword

sufuria. Metal cooking pot with narrow lip around the top

TANU. Tanganyika African National Union, Tanganyika's only political party.

tembo. Elephant

ugali. A stiff porridge made from maize meal

Being Mortal
Gawande

LaVergne, TN USA
29 September 2010
198957LV00006B/149/P